SEVEN
WORDS TO
CHANGE
YOUR
FAMILY
...WHILE THERE'S STILL TIME

SEVEN WORDS TO CHANGE YOUR FAMILY

...WHILE THERE'S STILL TIME

JAMES MACDONALD

MOODY PRESS
CHICAGO

Moody Press, a ministry of Moody Bible Institute,
is designed for education, evangelization, and edification.
If we may assist you in knowing more about Christ
and the Christian life, please write us without obligation:
Moody Press, c/o MLM, Chicago, Illinois 60610.

ISBN: 0-8024-3440-1

1 3 5 7 9 10 8 6 4 2

Printed in the United States of America

To my parents,
Verne and Lorna MacDonald,
who have a "Wow" marriage after forty-five years
and whose children have all risen up to call them blessed.
May we all build faithfully upon the truths you have so lovingly entrusted to us.

"The things which you have heard . . . entrust these to
faithful men who will be able to teach others also" (2 Timothy 2:2).

You have done this so well; now it's our turn.

CONTENTS

➤➤ ◄◄

FOREWORD

→→ ←←

I am so excited that the Lord has led James to put into written form these messages about family transformation. However, I must say that there is something very ironic about his writing a family book, because he seldom reads them. For years I have been the one reading everything I can get my hands on about parenting and marriage. I have put the best ones in front of James and am yet to see him "devour" them, as I love to. No, his credibility in writing this book is not his familiarity with all that has been written in the field. James knows about family issues only from his study of God's Word and from his passionate desire to see those truths work in our own home. I have the joy of witnessing on a daily basis what those outside our home will never observe: a man who has refused to allow the demands of a growing ministry injure the application of God's Word in our marriage and with our own children.

When I read a book on the family, the nagging question in the back of my mind is: "Does the author follow the counsel he is challenging me to accept?" In the case of *Seven Words to Change Your Family*, the answer is a resounding YES! What James has written are principles tested and proven in our own home.

I believe and will be praying that God will use them to enrich and strengthen your loved ones as well. May Jesus Christ alone receive glory for the transformation you will experience as you read, reflect, and implement these *Seven Words to Change Your Family.*

KATHY MACDONALD

ACKNOWLEDGMENTS

B y far the happiest part of book writing for me is this page. This is the people page. It's the page that reminds both the author and the reader what we
all must keep in mind: that life is not a solo or soliloquy. Life is a team sport;
it's a family affair, and no one can make it to the finish line without faithful
partners. Nowhere is this more true in my life than in writing a book.

This is my third book on the subject of change and my third opportunity
to thank the same people (with a few additions) for their same faithfulness. It
is deeply appreciated. Thanks to the people of Harvest Bible Chapel who support my preaching ministry, from which each of these chapters originated.
Thanks to all of our friends at Moody Bible Institute and Moody Press; you are
excellent partners in the Lord's work. Thanks to Rosa Sabatino, who took each
message from tape to transcript with punctuality and accuracy. Thanks to Dan
Brubacher, who edited each transcript from its verbal style to a written format with great attention to detail. Thanks to Jim Vincent at Moody Press and
my research assistant David Jones, who made the final edits when I was done
writing and greatly improved the end result. Thanks to Kathy Elliott, my personal assistant for more than thirteen years, who kept the entire team—including me—in place and on time.

Abundant thanks to my wife, Kathy, for standing with me for eighteen-plus years of family life. She has patiently partnered with me as I have tried and failed and tried again to put into practice the contents of this book. And to our three children, Luke, Landon, and Abby, who graciously allow me the freedom to talk about our family, warts and all. "I have no greater joy than this . . . my children walking in the truth" (3 John 4).

A special word of thanks to my informal family mentors through the years: Cliff and Barb Talbot, Marvin and Kay Brubacher, Doug and Carolyn Schmidt, Ted and Vicki Lewis, Dave and Betsy Corning, Ron and Sherry Allchin, and Joe and Martie Stowell. Watching your family live out the message of the Cross has made me a better husband and father and blessed my family as a result.

Most of all, thanks are due to our gracious God, who provides grace and truth in perfect balance so that we can try and fail and try again, and never stop changing into His likeness and for His glory. "And we saw His glory . . . full of grace and truth" (John 1:14b).

INTRODUCTION

⟶⟶ ⟵⟵

Why would you pick up a book like this? Is it because you sense the need for *change* in your family? If so, you are not alone. Family life is the bull's-eye of our existence. It's not practice for anything—it's the playing field, it's the hub, it's the main course, it's the coup de grace (not sure what that means, but it's big!). Family life is where our greatest joys and sorrows are experienced.

Family life is not the earning place and it's not the learning place, but it's the churning place where what we earn and learn is consumed. Family life is not the public place that generates praise and notoriety, but it's the private place that can drain public accomplishment of every ounce of satisfaction. Family life is difficult and draining if neglected, but it's delightful and dynamic if its demands for priority treatment are met.

Sad but true, most of us know firsthand that if life is not working at home, it's not working period—no matter how "successful" we may be in other places. No wonder our unseized thoughts so often drift toward home. It's only natural to dream and pray and study and work toward improvement where it counts most and yields the highest returns.

All that to say that if you're looking for "home improvements," you've come to the right place.

Let's Play a Game

Wanna play a little game? Come on; it will be fun, and I have a method to my madness. It's what we call a guessing game. I am not a prophet, and I am certainly not one of those cheesy psychic 900-number con artists, but I bet I can guess the reason you picked this book up. Really, I think I can. Need a prize? OK, how about this: If I can't guess why you're holding this book, then you win the freedom to put it down without hesitation and take back the time you would have wasted reading some dumb book by an author who "just doesn't get it." But if I can guess the reason you are interested in this book, then you have to read it and prayerfully apply its truth in your family. Are you in? I guess the reason; you read the book; I fail and off you go. Deal? I will need five guesses. Let's play!

Guess #1. Is your marriage hurting? Maybe the hopes of your wedding day have faded into more work and less WOW than you ever dreamed. Perhaps the seeds of neglect sown over months and years are now coming to fruition in emotional distance and an inability to communicate without anger and misunderstanding. Maybe your spouse is not walking with God as he or she should, and the fallout of the rebellion is affecting your marriage or your children. Did you pick up this book because you know your marriage needs help? If so, I've got good news: Help is on the way.

Guess #2. Are you concerned for your children? Maybe they are very young but already strong and willful. As you think about the future, you know that some things will need to change if your children are going to grow up to respect your authority and, more importantly, the Lord's. Maybe your kids are now in high school, and you see your influence declining at the very time you sense it should be on the rise. You wonder where some of the recent attitudes are coming from and know that a confrontation is on the horizon. Maybe your kids are now grown, and you see them making decisions that are far from the way you have taught. You want the Lord to use you, but you don't want to fracture the relationship. Did you pick up this book because your kids need help? Again, I have good news. God's Word has answers, and I am writing with your specific need in mind.

Guess #3. Has your family fractured beyond repair? Have you been through a divorce and the family that remains is detached and devastated? Maybe your children are grown and living so far from God that you can't imagine them ever coming back. Maybe you or someone you love has made an awful choice that has detonated an atomic explosion in your family—or will very soon. Is your family in pieces and you have no idea what to do or where to begin? Did you pick up this book because you need 911 for your family—now?! Not only will this book help you, but I believe that God Himself has led you to pick it up in answer to your prayers.

Guess #4. Is the problem outside your home but still in your extended family? Perhaps with your in-laws, or one of your parents, or a sibling? Maybe some words have been spoken that should have remained unsaid. Or worse, a crack in the family has grown into a communication canyon, and you have no clear idea how to get a message of love across the gap. Estrangement from extended family members can be both persistent and perplexing. Did you pick up this book because you desire better relationships with the family members who don't live at your address? Wonderful, because up ahead are some very practical things you can do to melt the ice and see a new springtime of warmth and affection burst forth among you and your loved ones.

Guess #5. Is your need less dramatic and more dripping? Is it less like a tornado and more like a leaky faucet? Are you burdened, not because of the gaping hole in the side of the ship, but because some smaller persistent things are secretly draining the joy and fulfillment from your family life? Are you looking less for a major overhaul and more for a good, solid tune-up? Do you need a focused review of the basics of a successful Christian family? Yahoo, I have been thinking about you, too! And if you do the things that are coming in these eight chapters, you will experience the family upgrades that you have been thinking and praying about.

CHANGE IS ON THE WAY

Good news! The purpose of *Seven Words to Change Your Family* is to bring significant change in the exact situations described above. If I touched on the situation motivating your interest, then it looks like we are going to be spending a few hours together. I'm sure you're a person of your word, so if I guessed your situation, then you're in . . . right? (The only ways I might have missed your reason for picking up this book is that you're reading for a loved one with a need like those listed above, or you simply love family books, in which case you would read it anyway, wouldn't you? ☺)

I know from experience that what's in the coming pages can bring lasting change to the very circumstances you're facing. In fact, I have been writing with some very specific needs in mind, and I believe you have picked up this book for a reason. We have been praying that God would use this book to bring healing and health to the family needs that are on your heart, and I believe He will if you follow through and read to the very end. Before we begin, I want to give an overview of what you'll be reading so that you'll have a clear sense of what you've signed up for and how to make the most of this opportunity for you and your family.

WORDS THAT CAN BRING TRANSFORMATION

The seven words up ahead are divided into three sections:

1. Three *healing* words, to help you conquer the pain of the past and get on a new page for the wonderful future God has in store for you. The healing words will minister to you and your family and help you know where to begin and how to "get the ball rolling," if you know what I mean.
2. Three *building* words, to help you put good habits in place of ones that may have been more negative. The building words will give you actual actions to implement and assist in your family's transformation. If your family needs a tune-up, focusing on these building words will help for sure.
3. One *transforming* word. There is something that you must have every step of the way. You can turn to it right away if you want, but it fits far better at the end as a covering for all the wonderful things I am trusting God will do for you and your family.

Each chapter begins with some content to introduce the key word. The substance of each chapter follows, teaching the specific word from Scripture in such a way that, if applied, can truly transform your family from top to bottom. Notice that I said, "if applied." There is in the church today a notion that simply hearing the truth brings transformation, but that is not the case. In fact, James 1:22 tells us that simply hearing and not applying the Word is self-deception. There is no value in *Seven Words to Change Your Family* apart from actually applying the truths you will be learning in active, specific ways. To help you do that, we are concluding each chapter with three application aids:

1. *A prayer to lift you higher.* Be sure to take seriously the prayer written out for you at the end of each chapter. Don't simply read it as my prayer, but take some time to kneel down, open your heart to God, and truly come before Him by faith. Prayer is an act of humility, and God gives grace to the humble. He loves it when we pray this way, and if you put your heart into the prayers at the end of each chapter, God will give you the needed grace to go to work on what you are learning.

2. *A project to take you deeper.* As helpful as it may be to read the work of another person (like you are doing now), experts agree that life transformation is far more probable if you put some of your own "elbow grease" into the process of learning. Every chapter conclusion will include some in-depth questions and suggested Scripture passages for further study on your own. If you allow the Word of God to speak to you in this way, the Holy Spirit will entrench much more deeply your commitment to actually put into practice what you are learning.

3. *A practice to take you further.* This is where the rubber meets the road. Up to this point, it has been just you all alone with these transforming truths, but now it's time to put them to work. The final sentences of each chapter will outline a plan of action for you to take—a way to put into practice the truths that you have been reading, studying, and praying about. I promise you with 100 percent confidence that if you take these action steps and move from illumination to implementation, your life and family will never be the same!

READY TO MAKE A COMMITMENT?

So what do you say? Are you in? Don't forget that if family transformation were easy, everyone would be experiencing it—but they're not. And the only reason you have read this far is because you really want God's best for your family. God wants it for you, too, but you'll have to be committed to make it all the way through. Some of the ground up ahead will not be easy.

Why not make a commitment right now? (Get a pen! ☺)

I (name) _Liesl Bell_____ do
promise before God that, with His help, I will not only read the chapters
of *Seven Words to Change Your Family* but will prayerfully complete the as-
signments and implement the truths I am learning so that my family will
experience God's transforming power.

(date) _10-8-05_____
EXCELLENT!

BEFORE WE BEGIN . . .

I know that you are probably anxious to dig into the first of the seven words, but before we do there is an opening chapter that must be covered. The word that we are starting with must precede the "change" words or they will have no impact. It's not a word that brings change itself, but it does fuel the desire to be changed. The word is *hope,* and it is one of the greatest needs in the families of our day. Someone has said that if you have lost hope, you have lost everything, and far too many families I meet and talk with have lost their hope. They are not seeking transformation; they are seeking survival. They are not believing God for a better tomorrow at home; they just hope to have a home tomorrow.

Maybe at this moment you are very discouraged about the needs you see in your family. Before we get to the change words, I want to encourage you and build within you a sense of hope. God loves you and is working today to bring lasting joy and transformation to your family. That's what He is doing every day in our world. In fact, Hosea 6:3 tells us that God's "going forth is as certain as the dawn." God wants to do a miracle in your family, and He wants to begin that work today through you. Unless you have hope, unless you believe that God can and will bring transformation to your family, the rest of the book will be a big waste of time. And so we're starting in chapter one on the subject of hope. OK? Turn the page, and let's trust God for a fresh new work of hope in our hearts.

HOPE FOR
THE FAMILY

⤞ ⤝

E veryone is talking about family. At parties, across the back fence, in the workplace, and in the secret places people are pouring forth about their families. Tragically, many of these countless conversations are filled with words of hopelessness.

As a pastor, I hear more than my share: "I just don't believe that my marriage can ever be different!" Or: "My son is so far gone—I can't see him ever coming back from where he is!" Or: "If you knew my sister, then you would understand why the kind of relationship I dream of having with her is an impossibility." Or: " I've tried to be close to my Mom, but it just hurts too much! I can't try anymore."

We all speak words we regret in moments of desperation and are tempted to say, "I don't mean that; I'm not sure where that came from," but in reality we know that the words came from within us. In Matthew 12:34, Jesus taught that **"the mouth speaks out of that which fills the heart."** If the heart is where true feelings reside, then the hearts of many are filled with despair about their families—feelings of fear that things will never change and thoughts of futility that another attempted turnaround will only lead to failure.

This is a sad situation for anyone, but especially for those of us who are followers of Christ. After all, we worship the almighty God who says, "Mark it down. I'm for the impossible stuff!" He's the One who said, "**Call to Me and I will answer you, and I will tell you great and mighty things, which you do not know**" (Jeremiah 33:3). God has gone on record again and again saying, "Do you know what? When it seems desperate, when it seems out of reach, when it seems like it could never be turned around—call on Me; I will answer you!"

In the chapters ahead, we're going to spend a lot of time learning what we can do to experience God's transforming power in our family, but there's little point in going any further if we don't believe that our family can actually change. Without hope we're wasting our time, and neither of us wants that, do we? The goal, then, for this chapter is that God would produce hope in our hearts—hope that our best days are not behind us, but that our happiest family times are still ahead. Hope is the heartfelt confidence that the most joyful moments in our marriage and with our children and grandchildren are not in the rearview mirror, but are just around the next corner. When I truly believe that the greatest days for my family are still in the future, I have hope.

HOPE IS PROMISED IN GOD'S WORD.

Scripture has so much to say on this matter of hope. Here are just a few of the passages the Lord has used to "stoke" hope in the furnace of my own heart:

> "**Why are you in despair, O my soul? And why have you become disturbed within me? Hope in God, for I shall again praise Him for the help of His presence.**" (Psalm 42:5)
>
> "**My soul, wait in silence for God only, for my hope is from Him.**" (Psalm 62:5)
>
> "**For You are my hope; O Lord God, You are my confidence from my youth.**" (Psalm 71:5)
>
> "**I wait for the Lord, my soul does wait, and in His word do I hope.**" (Psalm 130:5)
>
> "**'There is hope for your future,' declares the Lord, 'And your children will return to their own territory.'**" (Jeremiah 31:17)
>
> "**For whatever was written in earlier times was written for our instruction, so that . . . we might have hope.**" (Romans 15:4)

HOPE CAN BE STOLEN.

To truly build your hope for all the transformation up ahead, I can't just give you a pep talk. To have hope that our families can change, we must look at what steals our hope. Trust me, the message of hope is coming, but first we need a clear understanding of why our family stuff so often punches a hole in our reservoir of hope.

It's not the problems at work, or even at church, that drain our hope; it's the pain in our families. There is no pain like family pain. Family pain is the injury that hits the hardest, hurts the most, and lingers the longest. It can come from the sin of a prodigal son or the loss of a dear loved one.

I write this from recent personal experience. Last summer my grandmother passed away suddenly in a car accident. She was eighty-six years of age and the spiritual cornerstone of our family. She and my grandfather were born again in their early thirties and subsequently led my great-grandfather to Christ. For more than fifty years, my grandma followed Christ and studied His Word, but most of all, she prayed. She was a woman of prayer like I have *never* met elsewhere.

How many times I remember going to her big farmhouse and sitting down in this special room. Two chairs faced each other right in front of a big picture window. She would reach with both arms to grasp my hands, then close her eyes and begin to call out to the Lord for me, and then for my wife and children by name, always with specific prayer requests. Inevitably, as she would pray for five, ten, even fifteen minutes without stopping, I would open my eyes and see the tears running down one cheek. (My grandmother had only one eye as a result of a childhood illness.) I have countless memories of those prayer times.

After her wake, our entire extended family went back to her house and into that prayer room. The room contains several antique chests and tables, each with one or many drawers. We began to look through the drawers and discovered they were jammed to the top with scraps of paper. On each piece was a date and detailed prayers my grandmother had prayed in that room over the years for our family. Of course, it's only human nature to look for your own name and wonder what Grandma had been praying for in 1974 or whenever. I soon found several pieces of paper with my name on them and specific burdens I had carried through the years. Most of them were long ago forgotten by me but remembered before the Lord by Grandma—specific, articulate prayers for every child and spouse and fervent, visionary prayers for every grandchild and great-grandchild.

What a lasting legacy of prayer! I am sure eternity is going to show much more than I ever realized that the fruitfulness of my life—if there is anything praiseworthy in it at all—may be related far less to my efforts and far more to the faithfulness of my grandmother.

And so it has been a great loss. There is no pain in the world like that kind of pain. It attacks us at the very core of who we are and tempts us to doubt the goodness of God. Family pain assails our hope and tries like nothing else to conquer our hearts with despair.

THINGS HAVEN'T CHANGED MUCH.

You have your own story. You know firsthand that nobody can hurt us like the ones under our own roof. This is true in our time, and it was definitely true in Bible times. Consider the example of King David. By the end of his life, he had been through his share of highs and lows. He triumphed over Goliath, the Philistine warrior, but he experienced great persecution by King Saul. He became king after Saul's death and won mighty victories with the Israelite army, but later David fell into an adulterous relationship with Bathsheba and was confronted by almighty God through the prophet Nathan. David had experienced a lot, but his greatest pain was still ahead.

If family is the biggest pain target in our hearts, then our children are the bull's-eye. Nobody—and I mean nobody—can devastate you like your own kids. David learned this truth firsthand when his son, Absalom, turned on him and became rebellious. The episode itself is so sordid and sick that it sounds like the story line of a soap opera. It all started when Absalom murdered his half-brother as payback for raping his sister Tamar. Later Absalom became jealous of his father's popularity, turned his most trusted advisors against him, and chased David not only off the throne but also right out of the city of Jerusalem.

So there was David alone in exile, while the shattered remains of his army were out trying to defeat his own son. Ouch!

In 2 Samuel 18, two runners are seen approaching the exiled king to update him on the battle. The first one, afraid of the king's wrath, gives a lame, vague report. So David asks the second messenger, the Cushite, **"Is it well with the young man Absalom?"** (verse 32). He didn't care about the battle, he didn't care about the victory, and he didn't care about the throne. What he desperately wanted to know was, "Is my son OK?" Reading the story you want to say, "You mean the son that has been fighting against you? You mean the one who would kill you in a second if he had half a chance?"

The Cushite answered, **"Let the enemies of my lord the king, and all who rise up against you for evil, be as that young man!"** Gently stated but clearly communicated, David's treacherous son, Absalom, was dead.

No doubt everyone present held their breath as they waited for David's response. Verse 33 says, **"The king was deeply moved and went up to the chamber over the gate and wept. And thus he said as he walked"**—can't you see him pacing back and forth, wringing his hands?—'**O my son Absalom, my son, my son Absalom! Would I had died instead of you, O Absalom, my son, my son!'**" How can you explain that—David, the ruthless warrior, crying like a baby when his archenemy is finally defeated? It's very simple: The enemy was his own flesh and blood, and there is no pain like family pain. Those we love most are also those to whom we are most vulnerable.

MORE BIBLE FAMILY PAIN

The Bible makes no effort to candy-coat the pain families experience. Remember Noah, the man of faith? After the Flood, he planted a vineyard and became drunk. Genesis 9:21 tells us that he was naked in his tent. Why? We are not told; we can only imagine. His son Ham came along and saw the shame of his nakedness. But instead of covering him to preserve whatever dignity he had left, Ham went and told his two brothers (verse 22). When Noah learned what Ham had done, he flew into a rage and cursed Ham's son Canaan (verses 24–25).

Eli was a priest in the temple of the Lord. The Bible tells us that he was such a failure as a father that his own sons were stealing out of the offering and sleeping with women at what amounted to the front door of the church. First Samuel 2:12 describes them as **"worthless men; they did not know the Lord."** How Eli must have anguished over the fact that he spent his whole life serving God, yet he lost his own children! Family pain.

The prophet Hosea, who was called to speak for God, married a woman who became a prostitute. A picture of Israel's unfaithfulness to God, Gomer went out and slept with every willing man she could find. On two separate occasions, she came home pregnant. The first illegitimate child was called Lo-ruhamah, which means "not loved" and the second was called Lo-ammi, which means "not Mine." Just imagine the faithful prophet of God walking through the streets introducing his children. "I want you to meet my two kids, Not Loved and Not Mine."

It's absolutely heartbreaking! The Bible is not a retouched photo, and some of its saddest verses are family verses. The stories parallel our own lives and proclaim the truth: There is no pain like family pain.

THE STATS DON'T LIE

Family pain is so common in our day that it hardly needs description, but here are a few thoughts from current research:

- Thirty-four percent of married couples today in the United States have been divorced at least once.[1]
- Of Christians who have been divorced, 90 percent report that their divorce occurred after their conversion.[2]
- One popular magazine asked its readers, "Which would you rather have: five extra hours a week at home, or ten thousand dollars a year?" Eighty-three percent took the money.[3]
- For women between the ages of fifteen and forty-four, domestic violence is the most common cause of injury. Sadly, the church is not immune. Summarizing the studies, ten of every sixty women in a church are being abused verbally at home, and three of those ten are being abused physically.[4]
- More than a quarter of American children—nearly seventeen million—do not live with their fathers.[5]
- Almost one out of every three children born in the United States in our day is the child of an unwed mother.[6]
- The National Center on Addiction and Substance Abuse surveyed hundreds of kids between the ages of twelve and seventeen and found that only 25 percent reported living in a home where parents established and enforced rules. Three out of four live in homes with no rules, no guidelines, no deadlines, and no curfews. And out of that comes every statistic

related to dysfunction, from prolonged therapy to substance abuse to adult criminal activity.[7]

WHO'S TO BLAME FOR ALL THIS PAIN?

Now we know what drains the hope from our hearts, but what causes all this family pain? Clearly, family pain is all around us. You don't have to look far to find it. But why? If family pain is what drains the hope from our hearts, where does it come from? Well, at the risk of stating the obvious, all family pain is either directly or indirectly the result of *sin*.

IN THE BEGINNING

In the beginning, there was no family pain. God had created the entire universe—speaking into existence everything from the planets and stars to the earth itself, and every plant and animal that calls our world home—and it was good (Genesis 1: 31). Then He came to the crowning moment of creation and said:

> "Let Us make man in Our image, according to Our likeness; and let them rule over the fish of the sea and over the birds of the sky and over the cattle and over all the earth, and over every creeping thing that creeps on the earth." God created man in His own image, in the image of God He created him; male and female He created them. God blessed them; and God said to them, "Be fruitful and multiply, and fill the earth, and subdue it." (Genesis 1:26–28)

Adam and Eve had it made! There was no pain of any kind in the Garden of Eden, least of all family pain. They had a perfect relationship with God and each other because they were without sin. They had five-star accommodations, food on the table every day, and just a little work to do.

Every day Adam and Eve got out of bed and said to one another, "So what do you want to do today?" Adam would chorus in, "Let's be fruitful and multiply! I love that job!" And Eve was like, "Shouldn't you start naming the animals?" (Things haven't changed much, have they?) But the important point here is that there was no pain. That first family was living in perfect harmony.

STEPPING DOWN INTO SIN

In Genesis 3, however, everything changed, and as their spiritual descendants, we are still experiencing the fallout. Genesis 3:1 says, **"Now the serpent was more crafty than any beast of the field which the Lord God had made. And he said to the woman, 'Indeed, has God said, "You shall not eat from any tree of the garden"?'"** Notice that *God's Word is questioned*. That is the first step down in every family. We say, "I know what God said, but does He really mean it?" We question the clear statements of God.

And then in verses 2–3, **"The woman said to the serpent, 'From the fruit of the trees of the garden we may eat; but from the fruit of the tree which is in the middle of the garden, God has said, "You shall not eat from it or touch it, or you will die."'"** The second step occurs when *God's Word is distorted*. God never said they couldn't touch the fruit; He just said they couldn't eat it. They could coddle it all they wanted; they just couldn't consume it. How important it is to get God's Word right! We're in for deep trouble when we distort it and make God say things He never said.

From there things start going downhill quickly. **"The serpent said to the woman, 'You surely will not die! For God knows that in the day you eat from it your eyes will be opened, and you will be like God, knowing good and evil'"** (verses 4–5). Perhaps Eve doubted in her own mind: "But wait, I thought God said we *would* die." Satan declared, "No, you won't die!" Right out in the open, *God's Word is denied*—the third step.

We're headed for big-time family pain when we allow God's Word to be questioned, distorted, and denied.

The final step down occurs when *God's Word is disobeyed*. Notice verse 6: **"When the woman saw that the tree was good for food, and that it was a delight to the eyes, and that the tree was desirable to make one wise, she took from its fruit and ate; and she gave also to her husband with her."** Do you see in that verse the all-important words, "with her"? Where did we get this notion that Adam was at the office when all this happened? He was right there with her, and they sinned together. **"She gave also to her husband with her, and he ate. Then the eyes of both of them were opened, and they knew that they were naked; and they sewed fig leaves together and made themselves loin coverings"** (verses 6–7).

BIG-TIME FAMILY PAIN

Sin entered the world and with it came family pain. Adam and Eve disobeyed the direct commands of God, and the family fallout was immediate: *broken fellowship with God* (they went and hid); *shame* regarding themselves and their bodies (they covered themselves up); and *relational strife* (they blamed one another). God's judgment brought pain to the family: pain in their roles, pain in the man's work, and pain to the woman in childbearing. And all family pain—from that day to this one—results from the choice to sin.

I know that there are men and women reading this who feel so alone in their marriage. They're thinking, *This is it? This is what I got married for? This is what I have to look forward to for the rest of my life?* Distracted husbands. Detached wives. Distant relationships. Feeling so alone and, for the most part, suffering in silence.

Maybe you are strong as a couple but devastated by the weight of children who are making choices that break your heart. For others, it's financial burdens—"You have run up *how much* on your credit cards? You've got to be kidding me!" As I meet with families and try to help them, I have often thought, *How can a person do that?* The answer is plain and simple: It's sin. It's thinking that stuff will make us happier than God.

Maybe infidelity has scarred your home. Perhaps it's substance abuse, sexual addiction, or worse. Maybe it's just a thousand little things that could and should be so much better. And if the truth were told, you're asking yourself, "Can any of this ever change?"

HOPE STARTS RIGHT HERE.

Hope starts by calling my family problems *sin*. Until we are willing to call the issues in our home what they really are—*my* sin; *my* neglect; *my* avoidance of the issues; *my* refusal to live according to God's Word—we are not going to experience the grace of God for transformation. As long as we call it *weakness* when God calls it *willfulness,* we won't experience His grace. As long as we call it an *accident* when God calls it an *abomination,* we forfeit God's benevolence toward us. As long as we call it *indiscretion* when God calls it *iniquity,* we lose God's blessing.

We must be willing to pull the ugly thing—whatever it is—up on the table and face it honestly and openly and say, "You're right, God. It *is* what You said; it's sin! This pain in my family is because we've broken Your laws and forfeited Your favor." Only then will we experience God's life-changing power.

NOW FOR THE GOOD NEWS.

All in favor of good news? Here it is: God can cleanse your family sin. The family pain you may be feeling can be healed if you are willing to acknowledge its source and deal with it God's way.

You think your family has some issues? You think you all need some counseling, some help? Well, the family of God in Isaiah 1 was about as far out as you can get—so far out that God Himself was feeling disillusioned with them. The prophet Isaiah records the very thoughts of God in regard to His family. Let me just hit a few of the lowlights from chapter one. **"Sons I have reared and brought up, but they have revolted against Me. . . . My people do not understand"** (verses 2–3). God describes His offspring as **"evildoers, sons who act corruptly! They have abandoned the Lord . . . [and] despised the Holy One of Israel"** (verse 4).

Then in verses 5 and 6, God asks, **"Where will you be stricken again, as you continue in your rebellion?"** In other words, "I have had to spank you so many times to get you in line! There's not even a place anymore." **"The whole head is sick and the whole heart is faint. From the sole of the foot even to the head there is nothing sound in it, only bruises, welts and raw wounds."**

God is fed up! He says in verse 13, **"Bring your worthless offerings no longer."** In verse 15 He adds: **"So when you spread out your hands in prayer, I will hide My eyes from you; yes, even though you multiply prayers, I will not listen."**

Do you think that situation looks dark? Does it seem beyond hope? Then listen to what God says in Isaiah 1:18 as He reaches in love toward His wayward children. **"'Come now, and let us reason together,' says the Lord, 'Though your sins are as scarlet, they will be as white as snow; though they are red like crimson, they will be like wool.'"** Wow! It's the very same heart that's revealed in Exodus 34:6–7, **"The Lord, the Lord God, compassionate and gracious, slow to anger, and abounding in lovingkindness and truth; who keeps lovingkindness for thousands, who forgives iniquity, transgression and sin."** It's the very same heart that caused Micah to cry out, **"Who is** a God like You, who pardons iniquity and passes over the rebellious act of the remnant of his possession? He does not retain His anger forever, because He delights in unchanging love" (Micah 7:18).

I proclaim to you a God who is loving and forgiving and who wants—even more than you want—to heal the pain in your family. But it must start with an honest acknowledgment: "God, I need Your cleansing and forgiveness"; "I've not been the wife that You wanted me to be"; "I've not been the son that You wanted me to be, God"; "I've not been the daughter that I should have been. I've hurt my parents and I want to make it right."

NOBODY WANTS TO BELIEVE THE PROBLEM IS SIN.

Perhaps you say, "I'm a sinner; no doubt about it. But I just don't see how getting squared away with God is going to change things in my family. They're just too messed up!" Here's the deal: There is so much nonsense written today about the family. If I hear one more person tell me that the biggest issue in marriage is communication, I'm going to be sick! Everyone is talking about *fruit* issues when the *root* issue is always the same—it's sin. You say, "My husband just doesn't know how to communicate." Yet he goes out with his buddies and talks up a storm for four hours about some sports subject that interests him! His problem is not communication; it's pride. It's pride that causes men to starve their wives emotionally and find their affirmation from the workplace or their buddies. It's not that we don't know *how* to talk; it's pride that keeps us from opening up and making ourselves vulnerable and extending love.

Hope for the family begins when we get down to the root issue, and it's always the same. It's sin.

You say, "No. No, our problem is not sin; it's financial." But the deeper issue below the finances is a materialism problem, a spending problem. You think *stuff* can make you happy, but it can't—only God can. "We have sex problems" or "discipline problems" or "substance abuse problems." Do you want a surface makeover, or do you want life transformation? If you want the latter, then you have to get off the fruit stuff and get to the root stuff. Label that entire folder "sin." When you're willing to call it what it really is, God says, "Now you're getting it!" Then His grace will begin to flow into your life, and the change you have been longing for will begin to develop.

ONLY GOD CAN . . .

Only God can change our families. Psalm 127:1 is a favorite verse of mine, and I quote it often. **"Unless the Lord builds the house, they labor in vain who build it; unless the Lord guards the city, the watchman keeps awake in vain."** All your efforts, all your trying is completely in vain, unless you are linked in partnership with God. But if you and your family are linked in partnership with the Lord, then your best days are ahead.

Here is a preview of three things to expect when you commit to partner with God for His cleansing and transformation.

1. *This commitment to partner with God melts our pride.* "It's *me*, God. *I'm* the biggest problem in my family." Do you want to see God flow something great into your marriage? Before your head hits the pillow tonight, say to your spouse, "God's been teaching me some important things. I want you to know that I have been a big part of the problem in our marriage. Would you just pray that God will make me a better partner for you?" That melts pride. You say, "What if my husband or wife doesn't say it back?" Leave that with God. Be an instrument of God's grace in your home. James 4:6 says, **"God is opposed to the proud, but gives grace to the humble."**

2. *This commitment to partner with God cleans the slate.* A lot of people don't see transformation in their family because they're like, "Things are so messed up right now! How could God possibly turn this into a masterpiece? There's just too much negative to get beyond!" That's the grace of God. You can get on a new page. You don't have to build your future on the failures of the past. You can clean the slate. **"Though your sins are as scarlet, they will be as white as snow"** (Isaiah 1:18). You can begin afresh to be the man or the woman that God wants you to be for your family. Clean the slate.

3. *This commitment to partner with God releases His grace.* God wants to flow His grace and favor into your family. You might have said something to your wife a week ago, and normally it would have gone nowhere. But God will give you favor in her eyes. **"Humble yourselves in the presence of the Lord, and He will exalt you"** (James 4:10). When you link up in partnership with God, phenomenal things begin to come your way.

LET THE GOOD TIMES ROLL.

I can tell you for a fact that *nobody* at the end of life says, "Agh! If I could do it again, I'd spend more time at the office!" Nobody ever wishes he or she had given more time to hobbies and travel. Those are not the things that amplify joy and happiness. No, at the end of life, everyone always talks about the same stuff: their family, their spouse, and their kids. The apostle John said, **"I have no greater joy than this, to hear of my children walking in the truth"** (3 John 4).

Whether they are our physical or spiritual offspring, it's our family that brings us joy. It's the celebration of a son serving Christ. It's a daughter who is raising our grandchildren in the things we taught her. It is our Golden Anniversary. Those are the greatest joys of life, and they are worth fighting for.

HIS GRACE IS FOR *ANY* SITUATION.

My grandparents bought a cottage up in the Muskoka region of Ontario, Canada, back in 1960, the year I was born. When my father grew up, he bought his own cottage there, and then one of my brothers did the same. We have a little family compound right next to one of the premier Bible conferences in Canada, the Muskoka Baptist Conference. Our extended family has been attending there for as long as I can remember. For the last several years, I have had the great privilege of proclaiming God's Word at that Bible conference. I take a worship team from our church with me, and we minister in the morning and evening services for a week each summer.

This past summer was the first time that my grandmother wasn't sitting in the second row when I opened God's Word. Following a family wedding, Grandma set out alone on the four-hour drive Thursday morning to join us at the cottage and attend the final services of the week. (You say, "Why didn't somebody drive her?" Believe me, you couldn't tell her anything! She was going to drive herself.) As she was driving down the road, a car ran a stop sign and pulled right out in front of her. She never even touched the brakes. She was killed instantly and in the presence of her Lord.

By Thursday night, when Grandma hadn't arrived at the cottage, we were starting to wonder where she was. My dad sat on the porch for six hours, praying and waiting to see her come up that driveway. She didn't have a cell phone, so we couldn't call her. Just waiting, waiting, waiting. And as the sun went lower into the sky, we began to fear the worst. It was time for the evening service, and I had to preach. I was speaking on the Twenty-third Psalm. Immediately after the service was over, I rushed out of the chapel and my older brother came to meet me.

"Grandma is with the Lord," he said. I walked a couple steps across the parking lot, bowed my head, and wept quietly for a few moments. Incredible, painful loss.

But if you look for God's grace in any situation, you can find it. It was the first time in nine years that my entire family had been together at the cottage: *all* my brothers, *all* their wives, *all* their kids, *everyone* together—though we live so far apart. There was quite a scene, crying and praying and comforting and ministering to one another into the night. The next morning my dad pulled us all together and said, "Here is what Grandma would want." He led us over to her cottage, and we prayed together and talked about what her life meant and what we would miss about her the most. I certainly did not feel like preaching, but Dad felt Grandma would want us all to be in the chapel service. (It used to make her crazy if people came to the cottage and didn't go over to the conference grounds for chapel.)

In God's providence, my message that morning was from Psalm 23:4: **"Even though I walk through the valley of the shadow of death, I fear no evil, for You are with me."** I got up and preached my heart out. One of the phrases we studied was, **"He guides me in the paths of righteousness for His name's sake"** (verse 3), and how God guides the feet of His children into difficult circumstances so that we can proclaim the superiority of the life lived in God. He allows us to experience the hardest times so we can say for His glory, "God is faithful, and His promises are true."

When I came to the end of the message, I explained that "for His name's sake" is sort of the equivalent of raising a flag. We don't want to have *little* victory, half-mast victory; we want to have *big-time* victory, raising the flag to the top of the pole. We want to experience overcoming, super-conquering victory because of Christ who loves us. One of our worship team members began "raising the flag" by singing *It's All About You*, a song which proclaims everything as for the glory and fame of Jesus Christ.

Many of the several hundred people in the room had known my grandmother, and the presence of the Lord was being powerfully felt by all. I got up and I began to wave the Christian flag, symbolic of our commitment that these difficult **"paths of righteousness"** would be for **"His name's sake."** We were grieving, but we were celebrating.

Just then my younger brother, Todd, rose from his seat, walked right down to the front of the chapel, put his arm around me, and placed his hand on the flagpole. This may seem like no big deal, but it was huge because Todd had struggled spiritually for many years. For a long time, he was totally disinterested in the things of God, which was a great burden to all of us, perhaps to my grandmother most of all. I wouldn't embarrass him and give you the details because I love him very much, but let me just say that when he was in his twenties, he was so far from God it was like, "He is *never* coming back!" If you were to speak to him about Christ, he would get very angry and cut you off abruptly.

My parents and my grandmother fervently called out to God for him, and God in His grace got ahold of Todd's life and brought him back. In recent years, Todd has been growing very close to the Lord. But until that moment when he joined me in raising the flag, he had been very private about the recommitment of his faith. It was a mighty victory for him and for our entire family to see him go public in worshiping Christ. In fact, it was one of the greatest moments in my life. Real joy, family joy!

HOPE IS ALIVE.

I tell that story about my family because I want you to have faith to believe God for similar miracles of supernatural comfort and transformation in your family. Hope is alive when we are willing to believe that the sin problems which cause our family pain are within the reach of our loving and forgiving God. Hope is alive when we believe that the Lord desires to bring transformation to every part of our family, regardless of how dark or desperate the needs may seem this moment.

Psalm 42:5 says, **"Why are you in despair, O my soul? And why have you become disturbed within me? Hope in God, for I shall again praise Him for the help of His presence."**

A PRAYER TO GO HIGHER

Lord, thank You for the hope that is found in You alone. I need it so desperately today! Things aren't going the way they should in my family, and it is causing me much heartache and pain. I recognize that sin is the root problem, and I confess my own personal sinfulness. (Be specific.) I have not been the Christ-honoring family member that I could and should be. Cleanse me of my sin and make me right before You. Thank You for having a bright future in Your heart for my family. I choose to wait and trust You for it.

Lord, help me to live in Your grace and be filled with Your hope each day. I ask this in Jesus' precious name. Amen.

A PROJECT TO GO DEEPER

Someone has said that when you've lost hope, you've lost everything. It's true, isn't it? Take a few quiet moments to reflect on a time in your life when you had lost all hope. Maybe it was because of a painful family issue like we've been discussing. Perhaps it was an overwhelming hurdle at work. Or maybe it was an insurmountable financial struggle. Whatever the situation, journal your thoughts and feelings and emotions. What was going on inside you at that time?

Once you've done that, think about what made the difference. What moved you out of the pit? Jot some things down. Then go back to the beginning of this chapter and read the promises of hope from God's Word; then meditate on them. What can you take away from these verses to help you live in confidence and power this week?

A PRACTICE TO GO FURTHER

In the rest of this book, we are going to study how you can be an instrument of transformation in your family, but that is something you would never pursue without hope. Do you agree that family pain is the result of sin? Are you willing to turn to God in this moment and ask His forgiveness for your part in your family's pain? You may feel that the blame lies elsewhere, but there is no hope in that. God's work in your family starts in the places where you are willing to acknowledge your own failures. Right there in those places, God's work of transformation begins. What we confess God will cleanse, and what God cleanses He will work to transform. And the places where God is committed to transformation are the places about which we can confidently hope.

Take some time now and write down the things you want to see God do in your family, and then confess what you must do in each of those situations so that God's work of grace can begin afresh and you can experience hope.

Marriage Needs   **My Part**

_____   _____

_____   _____

Children's Needs   **My Part**

_____   _____

_____   _____

Parents' Needs   **My Part**

_____   _____

_____   _____

Siblings' Needs   **My Part**

_____   _____

_____   _____

NOTES

1. "Family," at the website www.barna.org/cgi-bin/pagecategory.asp?categoryID=20. Accessed on 5 December 2001.
2. "Born Again Adults Less Likely to Co-Habit, Just As Likely to Divorce," 6 August 2001, at the website www.barna.org. Accessed on 5 December 2001.
3. *Fast Company*, July/August 1999, 112.

4. Marlin Vis, "Battered into Submission"; on the Internet at "search illustrations"; www.preaching-today.com. Under the category "Domestic Violence."

5. "H.H.S. Fatherhood Initiative," HHS Fact Sheet, 18 June 1999. As cited at "search illustrations"; www.preachingtoday.com under the category "Fathers Needed."

6. "National Center for Health Statistics" *In Focus*, 10 November 1995. Cited at "search illustrations"; www.preachingtoday.com under the category "Births to Single Women."

7. Pete Hartogs, "Study: Rules Improve Parent-Child Relationship," www.cnn.com, accessed on 21 February 2001.

PART 1:
THREE
HEALING
WORDS

1. Forgiveness

2. Blessing

3. Honor

WORD #1:
FORGIVENESS

-+>- -<-+-

M y heart goes out to the family that is in a downward spiral. You know what I mean. Where every step forward is quickly met by two steps back. Where bad times and lonely times overwhelmingly outnumber the times of true joy. Where it seems like no matter how hard you try, the pain of failures past and the wounds of family conflict are just too close to the surface to get anything good going in a consistent way.

Do you feel like that? Do you find it hard to believe that your family can really begin to work well because your mind is filled with vivid pictures of times when it hasn't?

If so, you may have wondered to yourself, *What exactly can turn the corner for my family? What can break the cycle of neglect, confrontation, injury, and withdrawal, followed by even greater neglect?* If you're wondering how to heal the past and get some forward momentum going, the answer is without a doubt *forgiveness!*

I know you've heard that word before, but don't knock it until you have really tried it according to the principles of God's Word. Forgiveness is much easier to say than to accomplish, yet it is a God-given mandate that brings incredible healing. Please remember, we are not the People for the American Way; we are not the Rotary Club; and we are not the John Birch Society. We are the followers of Jesus Christ, and our Lord has commanded us to stay busy in this matter of forgiveness. How about a quick review of Jesus' teaching on the subject?

JESUS ON FORGIVENESS

In Mark 11:25, Jesus said, "**Whenever you stand praying, forgive, if you have anything against anyone, so that your Father who is in heaven will also forgive you your transgressions.**" In Luke 6:37, He stated, "**Forgive, and you will be forgiven**" (NKJV). In the Lord's Prayer, Jesus taught us to pray, "**Forgive us our debts, as we also have forgiven our debtors**" (Matthew 6:12). Wow! Are you ready for that? Those are some pretty significant statements. Where would you be if the Lord chose to forgive you *as* you forgive others? Somehow God is keeping track of the way that we forgive and the degree to which we forgive, and He is measuring His forgiveness back to us in the same portion. Yikes!

But Jesus didn't simply *talk* about forgiveness. He *modeled* it in His everyday life. From the woman caught in adultery (John 8:1–11) to His final words on the cross—"**Father, forgive them; for they do not know what they are doing**" (Luke 23:34)—Jesus was and is all about forgiveness.

How about you? If you profess to be a follower of Jesus Christ, are you all about forgiveness? No doubt there are countless people who have injured you; they have said false things about you; they have wounded you with their actions and reactions. Maybe the hardship came from a supervisor at work, or a neighbor across the street, or a teacher in school, but regardless of where it came from, the fallout from unforgiveness is huge. It's *huge,* and nowhere is this seen more clearly than in the home. So much of the anger and strife that exists in the family today is rooted in people's unwillingness to forgive.

DEFINING FORGIVENESS

I want to be really clear about what I mean by forgiveness. It's important for us to be on the same page if we're going to get anywhere, so here's our working definition. *Forgiveness is a decision to release a person from the obligation that resulted when they injured you.* Imagine for a moment that I dumped a bowl of breakfast cereal in my son's lap for no other reason than to aggravate him. Of course that would be wrong, and as a result of my choice to injure my son, there would be an existing obligation—in a sense I would owe him. I did something that was not right, and now I am in debt to him.

My son would be faced with two choices: Either he could become bitter and suffer over the wrong done against him, or he could release me from the obligation that resulted when I injured him. That is the essence of forgiveness—a decision to release a person from the obligation that resulted when they injured you.

WHEN FAMILIES DON'T FORGIVE

My prayer is that, as you read this chapter, God will reveal whom you need to forgive, the specifics of that forgiveness, and that you will then make a choice to forgive them. Are you up for the challenge? Great. Let's go to Matthew 18 and look at a story Jesus told about forgiveness. Keep in mind that the context of the passage is conflict resolution. Jesus had been teaching, in effect, "If you have a problem with somebody, work it out. If you can, just let it go. If you can't, go sit down with them and work it out. If they won't resolve the matter, take somebody along and try to work it out. If that bombs, get some elders from your church and pressure them to make the matter right." Nothing makes the Lord happier than to see His children living in harmony, so Jesus did a lot of teaching on this subject.

Peter was listening to all this teaching and no doubt began to think to himself, "But what if the person poured the cereal in my lap twice? What if he did it *seven* times? I bet I could probably forgive a person seven times." So he came to Jesus with a lot of confidence, thinking that he was probably in line for a Ph.D. in forgiveness.

"Then Peter came and said to Him, 'Lord, how often shall my brother sin against me and I forgive him? Up to seven times?'" (Matthew 18:21). He expected Jesus to say, "Wow, Peter, you are some serious forgiveness machine!" But instead Jesus responded, **"I do not say to you, up to seven times, but up to seventy times seven."** What's the math on that? Four hundred ninety times.

That's a lot of forgiveness! You may think, "Would somebody really do the same thing four hundred ninety times?" The point is, don't keep track. If you have a tally sheet on your fridge and you're at three hundred eighty-seven, you have a problem! Forgiveness is not to be measured or counted, but given freely.

DRIVING HOME THE POINT

To make His case, Jesus told a parable—a fictitious story that makes a point. **"For this reason the kingdom of heaven may be compared to a king who wished to settle accounts with his slaves"** (verse 23). This story is about "the kingdom of heaven," so we're talking about God's economy, not the world's economy. **"When he had begun to settle them, one who owed him ten thousand talents was brought to him"** (verse 24). One *talent* is roughly equivalent to a thousand weeks' labor—almost twenty years of work! Let me put that into perspective for you. The total annual tax bill for all of the provinces surrounding Jerusalem was nine hundred talents. The gold that went into the temple was worth about eight thousand talents. So a debt of ten thousand talents was more than a person could ever repay without winning the lottery or something. In today's terms, think of it as a *trillion* dollars, a massive amount of money—more than a person could ever repay.

The text continues, **"But since he did not have the means to repay, his lord commanded him to be sold, along with his wife and children and all that he had, and repayment to be made"** (verse 25). Of course they couldn't make repayment, so the king was basically saying, "Throw all of them into debtors' prison. Let's cash them out, cut our losses, get what we can, and move forward." **"So the slave fell to the ground and prostrated himself before him, saying, 'Have patience with me and I will repay you everything.' And the lord of that slave felt compassion and released him and forgave him the debt"** (verses 26–27). Amazingly, the king released him from the obligation.

"But that slave went out and found one of his fellow slaves who owed him a hundred denarii." In Jesus' day, a denarius was a day's wage, so the fellow slave's debt was a hundred days' wages. It was a significant amount of money, but compared to what the first slave owed the king, it was nothing.

The slave who had been forgiven the great debt was not very forgiving: **"And he seized him and began to choke him, saying, 'Pay back what you owe.' So his fellow slave fell to the ground and began to plead with him, saying, 'Have patience with me and I will repay you'"** (verse 28–29). It's déjà vu —same line as in verse 26. The guy who had been forgiven a trillion dollars is choking his friend for a bonus check! He was unwilling to forgive his fellow slave, and instead threw him into prison until he could pay back what was owed.

When the king found out about the slave's harsh action, he was enraged: **"'You wicked slave, I forgave you all that debt because you pleaded with me. Should you not also have had mercy on your fellow slave, in the same way that I had mercy on you?' And his lord, moved with anger, handed him over to the torturers until he should repay all that was owed him"** (verses 32–34).

The final verse of this parable, verse 35, is one you should circle in your Bible. Every family needs to know this verse. Jesus said, **"My heavenly Father will also do the same to you, if each of you does not forgive his brother from your heart."** Wow!

FOOLISH RATIONALIZATIONS

Jesus' story contains several principles that should bring us to the decision of forgiveness. First, notice that *the rationalizations used for not forgiving are foolish*. Peter was looking for a way out of forgiveness. He was looking for an excuse. "Lord, what if I forgive someone seven times? Is that enough? Can I go this far and no further? Is there a person I don't have to forgive? Is there a sin I don't have to forgive? Is there a point at which I don't have to forgive anymore? This forgive-everyone-everything-all-the-time stuff is just way too much! I need to put some limits on this forgiveness thing."

That's what Peter was looking for—a rationalization. Jesus responded, "No, you are to forgive everyone, for everything, all the time—unilateral forgiveness! Don't look for a way out."

Often this need to forgive is more apparent in others than in our own life and family. We see people and say, "Man, you need to forgive her!" or, "Dude, you really have to let that go and get on with your life!" The need to forgive is so obvious when it's another person's issue, but when the problem is our own, we struggle to make it happen, choosing instead to offer foolish rationalizations that won't stand up before God. Here are five of the most common rationalizations that we use to keep from forgiving—dumb excuses that we make that don't impress God a bit. Maybe you've used some of them yourself.

1. "The hurt is too big." That doesn't make any sense to me at all. Wouldn't you think that the *bigger* the hurt, the *more* that you would want to get

rid of it? It would seem that the little things would be the ones you wouldn't bother with. It's not the little burden we need to off-load; it's the big one that's weighing us down and crushing our joy. No, the bigger the hurt, the more we need to forgive.

2. "Time will heal it." How often I have heard people say this. Listen, time heals nothing. It might scar over, but you know it hasn't healed because when someone mentions the delicate subject or brings up the names of the people involved, you're like, "Agh! Don't touch that!" The pain is still very real because time is not healing it. You can be walking through the mall and come face-to-face with that person against whom you harbor unforgiveness, or you can be standing in the shower when all of a sudden a certain event comes to mind—and you know time is not healing it because it's still as painful as before. Time heals nothing.

3. "I'll forgive when they come and say they're sorry." Have you used that one before? If you have, here's a not-too-subtle news flash: They're not coming back to apologize! You say, "I keep waiting by the front door every day." Get a job! They're not coming. If you never forgive unless the people say they're sorry, you will hardly ever forgive. And even if they should come to make an apology, your unforgiveness will prevent you from being ready to receive them.

4. "I can't forgive if I can't forget." No, the reality is that you will never forget until you forgive. Forgiveness is both the crisis and the process of putting a person's sin behind you. It is setting it aside and saying, "I won't think about that anymore. I won't focus on that anymore." It's a choice that begins the process of forgetting. Unforgiveness binds the offense to your heart and ensures that you will never forget. Forgiveness is the first link in the chain of forgetting, not the reverse.

5. "If I forgive, they'll just do it again." Have you ever felt that way? I think those fears are very reasonable, especially when dealing with family members whom we can't avoid because they live with or near us. Forgiveness does not mean you have to put yourself at risk. (More on that later in this chapter.) Don't forget that unforgiveness is a burden. If there is a chance the person may wound you again, that is all the more reason to forgive. Otherwise you'll be carrying two burdens, either one of which is sufficient to destroy your life.

WATCH OUT FOR THE FALLOUT!

Notice something else from Jesus' parable: *The fallout of not forgiving is huge.* When you decide not to release a person but instead to nurse the injury and harbor the resentment, look out for some major consequences. You can see this so clearly in the life of the unmerciful servant. He must have been pretty good friends with the other guy for him to lend the servant what equaled four months' pay—and yet how close do you think they were after the unmerciful servant was finished choking him? So he shattered that relationship completely.

Most people know that unforgiveness leads to relational fallout and bitterness, but it can also lead to stupidity. How crazy was the unmerciful servant to throw his pal into jail? Yeah, that'll get the money back real soon! It just doesn't make sense. Why didn't he give the man a plan and help him work it through? Here's why. Because he didn't want the money back. He wanted something more than the money—he wanted revenge. He wanted payment in a different kind of currency.

That's what often fuels a heart of unforgiveness—a desire to see the other person suffer, to make them feel what they made you feel. You can walk down that road with your family if you want to, but believe me when I tell you, the fallout is huge.

The unmerciful servant also lost the respect of his fellow servants. Scripture says that they were "deeply grieved" at the way he was acting (verse 31). If you are harboring resentment and unforgiveness in your heart, I guarantee that there are people who don't want to be around you anymore because you are always negative and focused on the pain. They may not tell you that to your face; they will just vote with their feet, and you will wonder what happened to a lot of old friends. Watch out when your unforgiveness toward one member of your family begins to fracture your relationships with other members of your family.

Then there was the humiliation that the servant experienced before the king. Check out what he said when he was called back before the king—nothing! He couldn't speak a single word. The king said, "I forgave you *all* of this, and you can't forgive this *little* bit?" The servant was ashamed—utterly embarrassed. He couldn't spout a syllable.

Of course, who is the king in the story? God. Who is the servant in the story? Each of us. And we are headed for the very same appointment someday.

If we harbor resentment and unforgiveness, God is going to say, "I forgave you everything, and you couldn't even do *this?*" The fallout is huge.

BENEFITS OF FORGIVENESS

You might associate forgiveness with church sermons and lectures from when you were a kid, but researchers are currently finding links between forgiveness and health, both emotional and physical. The act of forgiving affects both the body and the mind. According to Everett Worthington, executive director of the Campaign for Forgiveness Research, the accompanying changes "will filter into your . . . facial expressions, body posture, and daily life. . . . It really reduces the hostility that a person has toward someone who harmed or offended him or her." He adds, "When people feel less hostile, . . . they tend to have fewer cardiovascular problems, fewer heart attacks, and to feel less stress. They don't get or stay as agitated. The less stress a person chronically feels, the better his or her immune system functions."[1] Forgiving people are more stable. They have stronger romantic and platonic relationships. People who forgive are often happier and less prone to depression and anxiety.

Recently, *Christianity Today* reported that former President Jimmy Carter, South African Archbishop Desmond Tutu, and former missionary Elisabeth Elliot joined together to raise ten million dollars for research into the physical and emotional benefits of choosing to forgive.[2]

Their support will further funding of projects that have been ongoing since the 1980s. Those studies have determined that people who forgive also tend to have fewer mental and emotional problems. Summarizing the findings, researcher and professor Glen Mack Harnden agrees with Worthington and notes these additional benefits of forgiveness: "It . . . heightens the potential for reconciliation, [and] also releases the offender from prolonged anger, rage, and stress that have been linked to physiological problems, such as . . . high blood pressure, . . . cancer, and other psychosomatic illness."[3]

These scientific findings showing physical and emotional benefits to forgiveness should not surprise followers of Christ. We serve the King of Kings and Lord of Lords who made us. He knows how our bodies work. Every time God says, "Don't"—as in, "Don't harbor unforgiveness"—what He's really saying is, "Don't hurt yourself." In other words, when you *choose to sin*, you *choose to suffer.* That's how things work in God's economy. So when God says,

"Forgive," it's like, "Do yourself a favor." When we fail to forgive, the fallout is huge.

LASTING CONSEQUENCES

Here's a third lesson found in Jesus' story: *The consequences of not forgiving are lasting.* Look at verses 34 and 35 once again. They are the most important by far in the parable. **"And his lord, moved with anger, handed him over to the torturers until he should repay all that was owed him."** First, unforgiveness is definitely torturous. If you refuse to forgive those who injure you, life will become for you a massive torture chamber where nearly every human encounter passes through the grid of your own unresolved pain. If you go through life like an umpire, keeping score and recording every offense, your time on this earth will only bring you heartache. If every time you are slighted or offended or sinned against you collect the issue in your "hurt bag," then sooner or later your bag will overflow and you'll need a dumpster. Before long your dumpster will overflow, and you will need a large truck to transport your unresolved garbage. If you continue living this way, you'll have to move to the dump and you'll wonder why you're so down in the dumps, when it's really just the torture and exhaustion of hauling around all the things you've been unwilling to forgive.

Meet adults who are living this way, as I often do, and by the time they are in their forties or fifties, they are so morose and miserable and medicated. Sad but true, God is still delivering people to the torturers because of their own refusal to forgive.

Notice also that the consequences of unforgiveness are experienced not only in this life, but also in the life to come. **"My heavenly Father will also do the same to you, if each of you does not forgive his brother from your heart."** And lest you write this off as an isolated reference, think again. This is not the only place where Jesus discussed the eternal consequences of failing to forgive. Matthew 6:14–15 says, **"For if you forgive others for their transgressions, your heavenly Father will also forgive you. But if you do not forgive others, then your Father will not forgive your transgressions."**

We live in a day when people often don't mean what they say. Parents raising their children warn, "If you do that one more time, you're going to get spanked." What happens? The child does, and the parents don't, and the kid quickly puts two and two together.

Imagine yourself walking down the street on your lunch hour with only a few minutes left, and you see Bob coming. You're like, *Uh-oh. There's Bob. I hope he doesn't see me!* But then he does see you. You say, "Hey, Bob. How's it going? Good to see you!" But you're not thinking that. Not really. You don't mean what you're saying, so you try to get out of it. You feel bad that you don't have the time to talk to Bob, so you say, "Bob, let's do lunch together sometime." Inside you're thinking, *Like never!* Do you know what I mean? In every human heart there is the sinful tendency to say things that we don't mean.

Now hear this: God absolutely means what He says. Every time! Completely! Without exception! He is not looking at Matthew 18 and saying, "Why did I write that? I am never going to do that!" No, God fully intends to do exactly what He said, and He will do it. Nothing will hinder Him.

James 2:13 reads, **"For judgment will be merciless to the one who has shown no mercy."** Are you ready to deal with that? God says, "You're going to be judged by the standard that you used with others." In fact, the person who over a lifetime refuses to forgive ultimately reveals that he or she has never really comprehended or received the eternal forgiveness that God offers in Jesus Christ. What cancer is to the body, unforgiveness is to the family. If you won't forgive, God won't bless or heal or restore or reach your loved ones.

[handwritten margin note: ? I need a longer answer to this]

FORGIVENESS IS NOT . . .

When some people hear about unilateral forgiveness, they are concerned, as Peter was, about appropriate limits and protections from people who injure us. I understand those concerns and want to take a moment here to explore a fuller understanding of exactly what we are and are not doing when we choose to obey God and forgive. So here are three things that forgiveness is not:

1. *Forgiveness is not enabling.* Suppose you said to me, "My mother has an overspending problem, and she always borrows money from me. She wastes my cash on foolish impulse purchases, and she is making me crazy!" Forgiveness does not mean that you have to drop by your mother's house with a few credit cards. "I'll show her how forgiving I am!" No, that is enabling a person to sin. Forgiveness does not require that you help the person do the thing for which you have forgiven them. That is enabling.

2. *Forgiveness is not rescuing.* Imagine that my sixteen-year-old son decides to take our family car out for a joyride. He steals the keys, takes off, and ends up driving the car up a tree. (Thank God we are only imagining that!) As a parent, I have a choice. Of course I must forgive, but forgiveness does not mean rescuing my son from the consequences of bad behavior. I don't have to try to bribe the judge or otherwise eliminate the repercussions that God may use to teach my son some important lessons.

3. *Forgiveness is not risking.* Let's pretend that my father becomes angry and violent when he drinks. (Sadly, some people live with this pain every day.) Every time he does, he really hurts me. Again I must forgive him, but that doesn't mean that I have to accept his invitation to the New Year's Eve bash. Do you see the difference? I don't have to put myself at risk for further personal injury. Forgiveness does not require putting myself in harm's way.

HOW DO FAMILIES FORGIVE?

Forgiveness comes in two parts. It begins with a decision, an act of my will. We call this the *crisis of forgiveness*. When I make the choice to release a person from the obligation that resulted when he or she injured me, I am completing the crisis of forgiveness. I am not looking for vengeance; I am not trying to get even; I am not wishing for bad things to happen to them; and I am not focused on their failure. In fact, I am not thinking about them at all. I've released them from all obligation that resulted when they hurt me.

Maybe you remember completing the crisis of forgiveness in the past, only to retract that act of grace and begin again to nurse and nurture the injury of someone else's sin. Maybe you have responded publicly in a church service and committed yourself to forgiveness, or knelt alone and promised God that you would forgive but fell into your old patterns of hate or resentment when you crossed paths with the one you had chosen to forgive. If that is your experience, you need to understand the difference between the crisis and the *process of forgiveness*. Beyond the crisis is the process of forgiveness, without which you will never experience the healing that forgiveness can bring. In the crisis of forgiveness we say, "I choose to forgive," but in the process we say, "I will treat you as though it never happened." Here is how that process works:

1. I won't bring the offense up to the *person,* except for his benefit;
2. I won't bring the offense up to *others;* and (hardest of all)
3. I won't bring the offense up to *myself.* I will not go over it and think about it and dwell upon it.

When you are doing that effectively, you are succeeding in the process of forgiveness. This is a lesson that I am learning little by little in my own life. I could share several acts of forgiveness that I have been working on for ten or fifteen years. I am still in the process. Praise God, I am doing a lot better than I was ten years ago. But here is the key: When I fail in the process, I have to go back to the crisis. If you do that faithfully, you will get free.

FAILING IN THE PROCESS

I was driving along with my oldest son, Luke, recently and we passed by a restaurant. He said, "Dad, how come we don't eat there anymore?" I could hardly believe what came out of my mouth: "Because I used to eat lunch there a lot with somebody who really hurt me! I don't like the person anymore, so I don't like the restaurant anymore."

That comment was a failure in the process of forgiveness. I brought up a matter about which I had forgiven someone, and not only reviewed it myself but communicated it to someone else. In that instance I was the one who was sinning. To make that right I needed to return to the crisis of forgiveness and say, "Lord, forgive me for dwelling on the failure of that person. I have forgiven them, Lord. Forgive me for my sin. You have forgiven me so much. How can I fail to forgive others?"

Later that day I had to return to the crisis and then begin afresh to live in the process of forgiveness: I won't bring it up to you, except for your benefit; I won't bring it up to others; and I won't bring it up to myself.

CHEAP GRACE AND THERAPEUTIC FORGIVENESS

There are some who teach that we must not forgive unless a person repents. They often point to Luke 17:3: "**If your brother sins, rebuke him; and if he repents, forgive him.**" This passage is wrongly used to teach a delayed form of forgiveness that somehow releases bitterness and yet withholds the actual act of forgiveness until the offending party repents. Those who espouse this position use several arguments that must be countered here. It is said, for example, that unilateral forgiveness does not mirror God's pattern (Ephesians 4:32), where He forgives us only when we repent. However, that is simply not so. In Christ we are forgiven "before the foundation of the world" (Ephesians 1:4), and at the moment of repentance God simply communicates to us by His Spirit what was accomplished in His heart entirely by grace before we were ever born.

Additionally, we are told that unilateral forgiveness is selfish. Said another way, a commitment not to bring the matter up to the person necessitates waiting until they repent; otherwise, we are forgiving only for our own sake and failing to work for the offending person's good. Again, the idea is that we must mirror the way God forgives, who does not remind us of our sin once He has forgiven. In reality, however, God does bring to our attention sin that He has forgiven when it is to our advantage to be reminded. Further, biblical phrases that describe our forgiven sin as being "in the depths of the sea" mean only that when God forgives, He does not hold our sin against us. For example, if a man is struggling with lust he may have experienced the Lord's complete forgiveness regarding past failures, and yet the Holy Spirit will remind him of that sin at a point in time lest he act unwisely in a particular situation and fall into that sin again. That's why I prefer to add the phrase "except for their benefit" to the process definition, and thereby truly mirror the way God forgives.

More than nine out of every ten New Testament passages dealing with forgiveness call for unmeasured, instant, unilateral forgiveness. I believe that when all biblical passages on forgiveness are reconciled, it is best to understand Luke 17:3 as talking about *communicating* forgiveness. In other words, do not verbalize to your brother the forgiveness you have granted until he sees his own sin and repents.

Beyond the point of when to forgive, there are some who teach that forgiveness for the sake of personal release from bitterness and anger is selfishly motivated, and that it is somehow more loving to hold off on forgiveness until the person repents. In reality, the personal benefits of unilateral forgiveness, when weighed against the emotional and spiritual fallout of unforgiveness, are the very motivations that the Holy Spirit inspired the New Testament writers to highlight. It is neither selfish nor "therapeutic" to embrace the benefits that God attaches to our obedience.

Forgiveness begins with a crisis and continues through a process. When I fail in the process, I must return to the crisis. In time I will begin to experience the incredible healing and blessing that God grants to the life of the truly forgiving person.

BUT WHEN WILL I SEE THE BLESSING?

Because our hearts often mislead us, people will sometimes ask me, "How can I know if I have truly forgiven someone?" To answer that question, let's look at Ephesians 4:31–32, where the apostle Paul writes, **"Let all bitterness and wrath and anger and clamor and slander be put away from you, along with all malice. Be kind to one another, tender-hearted, forgiving each other, just as God in Christ also has forgiven you."** In these important verses, we see both the fallout of unforgiveness and the blessings of true forgiveness.

First, when you forgive, *damaging emotions are eliminated.* They are decreasing in your life. You say, "What damaging emotions?" There are six of them in Ephesians 4:31. Do you see them in the text above? Let's go over each word:

1. *Bitterness.* The Greek word translated as "bitterness" carries the idea of cutting, and cut it does. Bitterness cuts our insides to ribbons. It is the fretting, irritable state of mind, the perpetual animosity that inclines a person to a harsh opinion of others. Bitterness is the sour, crabby demeanor. It's acid on the heart; it's a scowl on the face; it's venom in the words. So many people are so bitter! Why? Because they have failed at the point of forgiveness. Maybe bitterness isn't your issue. Maybe you're just wonderful most of the time. Maybe for you the problem is . . .

2. *Wrath.* This is a deeply settled indignation that flows from constant unresolved issues. Wrath makes the heart like a furnace. The more you stoke it, the hotter it gets—but always simmering, always burning just beneath the surface. This is a little different from . . .

3. *Anger.* Anger is a temporary excitement, an outburst of rage. It's the fist through the wall, the broken glass. Bang! It explodes and dissipates. Anger frequently shows up in partnership with . . .

4. *Clamor.* Clamor is the noise of relational strife. It's the loud self-assurance of the unforgiving person who requires everyone to hear their grievance. Clamor is hold-still-you're-going-to-hear-me-on-this-whether-you-want-to-hear-it-or-not. It's a damaging emotion, a symptom of unforgiveness. Then there's . . .

5. *Slander.* Slander is the depth of evil speech. It comes from the Greek word often translated "to blaspheme." And not just against God, but against others as well. Slanderous words are cool, calculated words intended to injure. Slander is the ready-aim-fire, I'm-going-to-say-this-and-I-don't-care-who-it-hurts. You may have wondered why people are like that. It's because of unforgiveness in their hearts. And finally . . .

6. *Malice.* Malice is the evil inclination of the mind, the capacity to locate wrongdoing and do it. It means literally "bad-heartedness." Malice says, "I am going to feel this. I am not going to let go of this. I don't care what you say. I have every right to feel this way!"

If any of these emotions are present in your life, you are destroying yourself. You're ripping a swath of destruction like a tornado across a Kansas wheat field. Worse, you are doing it to the people who love you, those closest to you. But when you choose to live by forgiveness, damaging emotions are gradually eliminated from your life.

Second, when you forgive, *healing efforts are renewed*. Verse 32 starts off by saying, "**Be kind to one another.**" The word translated "be kind" is not a general comment about how you should treat your favorite people; it doesn't mean, "Be nice to the people you like." In the context it means, "Be kind—without reservation—to the very people that you had to forgive." It's a fruit of forgiveness, and it's an action that reveals a heart change. Kindness when forced from an unforgiving heart only produces more anger. Have you ever been unforgiving toward your boss, and he didn't even know it? And then he comes by and asks, "Hey, would you mind helping me with a few of these things? I am so swamped!" You're like, "I cannot *believe* he is asking me that *again* today!" You probably won't tell him, but your attitude reveals that something is not right in your heart. You can't freely show kindness to that person. Where the capacity to show kindness is lacking, you know for sure that unforgiveness is lurking somewhere in the shadows.

Third, when you forgive, _healing attitudes are restored_. That is the word "tender-hearted." Tenderheartedness is a willingness to feel the pain of another. You say, "I would never feel that person's pain. No way! I would rejoice in their pain!" That's unforgiveness. But when you are ready to empathize, you'll begin to think, _Well, as awful as the sin was, they must have been hurting really badly, too, to have done that to me._ When you begin to open your heart up to the pain of the other person, when you have a growing capacity to be tenderhearted toward the one who injured you, forgiveness is well under way.

Finally, when you forgive, _Christ's example is elevated_. "**Be kind to one another, tender-hearted, forgiving each other, just as God in Christ also has forgiven you.**" Just like Christ forgave you. That's how we forgive—just like that. Just as fast. Just as freely. Just as fully. Just like Jesus. That's the way we are commanded to forgive.

HERE'S THE BOTTOM LINE FOR YOU AND YOUR FAMILY.

The bottom line is: There are no enduring relationships without forgiveness. I'm sure that you have a lot of dreams for your family. You will never see those dreams realized without forgiveness. There's no way around it. If you want to make it to your golden wedding anniversary, it's going to require several major forgivenesses and a truckload of minor ones. If you can't deal in the forgiveness environment, then you will have a lot of pain in your family's future. But here's the good news: You can forgive. And God wants to help you. Never are we more like Christ than when we choose to forgive.

The time to forgive is now, and it starts with a decision. You can't succeed in the process of forgiveness until you come to the crisis. Who is the person whose face has been in your mind's eye as you've been reading this chapter today? Is it a parent? A brother or sister? Maybe your child has hurt you and hardly even knows it. Make a choice to forgive. Maybe you need to write a letter this week. Maybe you need to make a phone call.

Make a choice to forgive. Tell the person, "I choose to release you from the pain that resulted when you injured me. You don't owe me anything. I forgive you."

One of the things that I've learned in almost twenty years of ministering to people (and I have seen it in my own life as well) is that *my capacity to forgive is directly related to my comprehension of how much God loves me.* When my concept of God's love is very small, my capacity to love others is very small as well. Paul said, "Christ's love compels us" (2 Corinthians 5:14 NIV). So often I see that the Lord's people need to have a breakthrough in their understanding. God doesn't love like our parents. God doesn't love according to our human experiences. God loves fully and unconditionally. That's what we're after.

A PRAYER TO GO HIGHER

Lord, thank You for Your example. I acknowledge that I am far less like You than I desire to be. Your example of forgiveness is so strong and so clear and so pure. Lord, often I am so small and so petty, and it injures both me and those I love. I pray that You would bring before my mind the names of people against whom I am harboring resentment and unforgiveness, especially family members. Maybe from this past week, or maybe from many weeks and months gone by, bring them to mind.

Lord, I pray that by Your Spirit You would give me the grace and the faith to believe that Your ways are best and to choose with my will to forgive. Strengthen me to do what I know is right. In Jesus' precious name, I pray. Amen.

A PROJECT TO GO DEEPER

Forgiveness is a common theme in both Jesus' personal life and His teaching ministry. Look up the following passages from the four Gospels, each of which gives additional insight into Christ's outlook on forgiveness: Matthew 6:12, 14–15; Mark 11:25–26; Luke 23:33–43; John 8:1–11. What observations can you make from these verses? Write down the things that jump out at you. But don't let this be just a "head exercise." What personal application can you make for your own life? How should you live differently because of these truths?

A PRACTICE TO GO FURTHER

Get a pad of paper and a pen, and spend some time kneeling before the Lord. Prayerfully ask Him, "Whom do I need to forgive? Against whom am I harboring sinful feelings of bitterness and unforgiveness? Search my heart, Lord, and reveal these people to me." As God brings them to your mind, write their names down on paper. Beside each name, jot down the specific thing(s) the person did to injure you, and also note how his or her actions negatively affected your life. One by one, declare your forgiveness (that's the crisis) for each person and every action on the page. Then ask the Lord to give you His strength to live out the forgiveness (that's the process) moment by moment.

Notes

1. Robert Owens Scott, "The Practice of Forgiveness," on the Internet at www.spiritualityhealth.com/newsh/items/article/item_2906.html. Accessed on 5 December 2001.
2. Gary Thomas, "The Forgiveness Factor," *Christianity Today*, 10 January 2000, 38.
3. Ibid.

CHAPTER THREE

WORD #2:
BLESSING

⇶ ⇷

Deep within the heart of every person is a longing for parental approval. We search for it our whole lives. If we don't receive it from our parents, we search for it elsewhere, and our hearts are restless until the blessing is found. When we do receive the blessing, our lives take on a level of fulfillment and security that cannot be realized any other way.

Now in case you were wondering, *blessing* is not some new psychological construct. It's been around for a long time. In fact, it shows up in the very first book of the Bible. Do you remember a guy named Abraham? After about two thousand years of Adam's descendants choosing sin over fellowship with God and submission to His laws, God decided to focus in on one nation to see if the people would choose the path of obedience. Abraham was the man God chose to be the father of this new nation.

The Blessing of the Birthright

Abraham had one miraculous son named Isaac; later Isaac had two sons, Jacob and Esau. Esau was born first and, according to the customs of the day, the substantive portion of the family wealth belonged to him; this was called the birthright. However, Isaac's wife, Rebecca, had a different plan in mind.

She favored the younger son, Jacob, as mothers will often do, and so she and the "baby" conceived a plan to trick Isaac into giving his blessing not to the firstborn Esau but to him.

Genesis 27:30–32 records what happened next:

> Now it came about, as soon as Isaac had finished blessing Jacob, and Jacob had hardly gone out from the presence of Isaac his father, that Esau his brother came in from his hunting. Then he also made savory food, and brought it to his father; and he said to his father, "Let my father arise and eat of his son's game, that you may bless me." Isaac his father said to him, "Who are you?"

That may seem like a strange question for a father to ask of his son— "Who are you?"—but earlier in Genesis 27 we're told that Isaac was very old and his eyesight was poor (no contacts back then!). So Esau answered:

> "I am your son, your firstborn, Esau." Then Isaac trembled violently, and said, "Who was he then that hunted game and brought it to me, so that I ate of all of it before you came, and blessed him? Yes, and he shall be blessed." When Esau heard the words of his father, he cried out with an exceedingly great and bitter cry, and said to his father, "Bless me, even me also, O my father!" And he said, "Your brother came deceitfully and has taken away your blessing" (verses 32–35)

Hear the heartbreak that is contained in Esau's cry—a great and bitter cry—"Bless me, even me also, O my father!" Later Esau cried out again to his father: "'Do you have only one blessing, my father? Bless me, even me also, O my father.' So Esau lifted his voice and wept" (verse 38). Keep in mind that Esau was not some soft, effeminate, emotionally fragile man. Far from it! He would have fit nicely on the cover of *Outdoorsman* magazine. Esau was a fisherman, a hunter, and a gamesman. The Bible even goes out of its way to say that Esau was a very hairy man (see Genesis 25:25, 27). So, in modern parlance, we would say that Esau was a "manly man." And yet, as a grown adult maybe forty years of age, he wept like a baby because his father did not give the blessing to him. We can learn a lot from that.

WE ALL LONG FOR THE BLESSING.

Each of us is far more like Esau than we might want to admit. Yes, deep within the heart of every person is a longing for parental approval. We want to feel confident that our mother and father know us, love us, and value us, that they are proud of us and recognize our accomplishments. From the preschooler who calls out from the sandbox, "Dad, look what I made," to the young child who fidgets nervously as Mom reads the report card and sees the latest grades, to the high school student who appears in the kitchen dressed for the prom and says, "How do I look?" to the grown adult who can't wait for Mom and Dad to see the new house, the new car, or the new baby—parental blessing is a universal longing.

I've heard some people say, "I don't need the blessing; my parents didn't give it, and I wouldn't receive it if they did." Yet I've watched those same people be absolutely transformed when they did receive the blessing. Almost instantly, they moved from a place of insecurity to one of confidence. I've heard someone say, "I wouldn't let my old man give me a nickel. In fact, I can hardly stand to look at him!" And yet I've watched that same individual get on a plane and rush across the country to plead for a word of love and commendation at his father's deathbed. I tell you again: There is something within the heart of every person that longs for the blessing. Our Father in heaven made us that way.

WHAT IS THE BLESSING?

But what exactly are we talking about? What is this blessing and in what form does it come?[1] The blessing is *a formula of words that expresses fondness for, confidence in, and recognition of a specific person.* In Old Testament times, the blessing was a bestowal of favor and acceptance, a transaction that gave material and spiritual benefit to the recipient. It was rooted not merely in a child's appearance or accomplishments, but in the child's very personhood. Though in some sense the blessing was given informally to the child as he or she grew up, there was a point in time in every Jewish family for a formal blessing ceremony. And while emphasis was placed on the firstborn, every child received it.

The Hebrew father would call together some of his peers, and they would gather in a circle around the son or daughter being blessed. (By the way, we see both males and females getting the blessing, though there seems to be within men an even greater need for it.) Normally, the ceremony would take place sometime between the ages of fourteen and sixteen. Each adult would bring a message of insight and practical wisdom filled with faith and conviction to share with the one being blessed. These messages were intended to form a foundation upon which the young person could build his or her future.

When the process was complete, the father would awkwardly lift his teenage child onto his shoulders and dance about the room in celebration. In effect, he was saying in front of his peers, "This is my beloved son (or daughter) in whom I am well pleased." That ceremony was the high-water mark, but equally important were the countless little blessings that were given day to day. And the blessing did not originate in Genesis 27 with Isaac. Scripture records that God blessed Abraham; Abraham blessed Isaac; Isaac blessed Jacob; Jacob blessed his twelve sons and two of his grandsons.

You might remember the story in Mark 10 where the little children were coming to Jesus. His disciples said, "Hey, Jesus is too busy. He doesn't really have time for you." **"But when Jesus saw this, He was indignant and said to them, 'Permit the children to come to Me; do not hinder them. . . .' And He took them in His arms and began blessing them."** (10:14, 16).

Now some of you may be saying to yourself, "Look, James, before you go any further, I already know that I didn't get this from *my* parents." Maybe that's true. But if life in Christ is about anything, it's about breaking the chains of the past. As you become an adult, you have to move beyond the what-did-I-get-from-my-parents mentality and recognize that your parents may have not received the blessing either. I am so thankful to God that I have the privilege of being a fourth-generation follower of Jesus Christ, and I am hugely grateful for a great-grandfather who said, "It starts with me." Perhaps you're the first-generation Christian who can draw a line in the sand and declare, "The blessing is going to start with me." What an opportunity God has given you! *You* can break the chains of the past! You can be the first in a line of people who will do the things that God in His Word has commanded be done.

Perhaps you're a single adult or married with no children, and you are saying, "I don't have kids of my own." But how many children are in your life? How many children are sitting at your feet whose parents don't have the wisdom to make sure their children get this blessing? Surely, every adult has some access to children and could meet this God-given need that every person longs to have fulfilled.

Phil's story about James being uncomfort- as a baby being held by Phil able when held by Phil b/c Phil was uncomfortable since w/ affection since James is a boy.

HOW CAN WE COMMUNICATE THE BLESSING?

You may wonder, *How do I communicate this blessing?* Here's the five-step process by which every parent can make sure the blessing is regularly and powerfully communicated to his or her children.

1. MEANINGFUL TOUCH

Back to Genesis 27. Notice in verses 26 and 27 how Isaac gives the blessing to Jacob. Scripture says, **"Then his father Isaac said to him, 'Please come close and kiss me, my son.' So he came close and kissed him."** Jacob is forty years old or more, and his daddy is kissing him. I love it! I could spend some time tracing the history of physical displays of affection in our Western world, but let me just give you the bottom line: When it comes to demonstrating affection physically, most of us are severely constipated. It's kind of tragic when a boy just thirteen or fourteen years old is uncomfortable expressing affection to his father. Or maybe the father is so stiff that he can't even get it done when the children are small.

Much has been written about the healing, nurturing, and affirming power of touch, and it's so sad when this is neglected in the home. Studies show that meaningful touch can lower blood pressure, protect our children from seeking sexual intimacy prior to marriage, and add up to two years to one's life.[2]

In recent years, a doctor carried out a study in a local hospital on the ways in which meaningful touch impacted his clients. Each day he saw a large number of patients, and he divided them into two groups. For the first group of patients, he would stand back and be very remote and distant. He would walk into the patients' rooms and speak very fact-of-the-matter: "Yes, your tests are back," and, "We won't know until tomorrow," and, "Here is your medication." He would make notes on the clipboard and walk out the door.

But with the second group of patients, the doctor would draw close to them, sit on the edge of their bed, and reach out and place his hand on their arm or leg. With great kindness, he would ask, "How are your feeling?" and, "How are you doing?" All of the patients, upon leaving the hospital, filled out a survey evaluating the care they had received. Without exception, the patients who had experienced the meaningful touch reported that the doctor had spent twice as much time with them, though in reality he had spent no more time with them than with those to whom he was very distant and reserved.[3] What a powerful example of how meaningful touch can communicate love.

Marilyn Monroe has been paraded before us as an example of someone who searched for, but seldom found, the joy of a lasting, loving relationship. What we are rarely told is that this tragic life had an even more pathetic childhood. Marilyn never had a home of her own, but was bumped around from foster home to foster home and from house to house. Many years later, an interviewer asked Marilyn, "Was there ever a time in your life, as you passed from family to family, when you felt loved?" She responded, "Once, when I was seven or eight. The woman I lived with was putting on her makeup, and I was watching. She was in a happy mood, so she reached over and patted my cheeks with her rouge puff." With tears in her eyes, Marilyn Monroe said, "For *that* moment, I felt loved by her."[4]

Dr. Ross Campbell noted the consistent report that men and women in prostitution began their involvement with a desire to be touched and held, adding: "In all of my reading and experience, I have never known one sexually-disoriented person who had a warm, loving, affectionate father."[5] Yet we offer such lame reasons for not touching our children in meaningful ways. You've heard them, haven't you? Here are a few:

- "I show my love by my actions." That is *so* lame! As if communicating love and blessing to our children is a show. Is each kid supposed to be a mini Sherlock Holmes, putting the pieces together: "I think he might love me, but I'm not sure"? Listen, there should be nothing subtle about this! A kid should not have to connect the dots to get a message of love and affection from his or her parents. Our child's life is to be immersed in love, acceptance, and blessing.
- "It makes me feel uncomfortable." If touching your children in ways that make them feel loved and affirmed is hard for you, it's probably because you did not receive such physical affection from your parents. May God help us to break those patterns of neglect and be everything that He has called us to be for the children in our lives.
- "It's not that important. I can make it up to them in other ways." When I hear parents make this excuse, I start to get mad. I'm not asking you to cut off your right arm here; just use your arms and your eyes and your

lips to send—without words—a life-changing message to your kids. And it's not just important for your two- and three-year-olds. It's important for your twelve- and thirteen-year-olds, and it's important for your twenty- and thirty-year-olds. I can't emphasize too much how very important this is.

- "I don't want to go overboard." Danger, sarcasm ahead: Yeah, I can't tell you how many times I've heard the testimonies of adults who say, "I am *so* messed up because as a kid my parents just slobbered all over me!" Have you ever heard that testimony? I have never heard that. "I am so messed up! I just can't deal with life because Mom and Dad used to hug and kiss me so often they just made me crazy!" As if!

2. SPOKEN WORDS

Here's the second part of the blessing: spoken words. A blessing is not a blessing until it is spoken. The most powerful way to build upon the foundation of meaningful touch is through the words you say to your children. The Scriptures tell us: **"Death and life are in the power of the tongue"** (Proverbs 18:21), and **"The tongue is a small part of the body, and yet it boasts of great things"** (James 3:5).

In our homes and with our children, the tongue has the power to destroy. How many adults are still struggling because of the angry words they heard as children? "You idiot!" "You are so stupid!" "I'm sick and tired of . . ." "You'll never learn, will you?" What parent hasn't said things they later regret? But while the tongue has the power to destroy, it also has the power to enrich and edify. Our words can build up and bless those we love. Here are kinds of words that should ring out relentlessly in the hallways of our homes:

1. *Words of affection.* Over and over and over in our homes, the words, "I love you," should be spoken. From husband to wife, from wife to husband, from children to parents, from parents to children. I have no respect for the man who reportedly told his wife, "I told you I loved you the day I married you, and if I change my mind I'll let you know." How stupid! "I love you" should be the constant refrain in the beautiful music our families make together.

2. *Words of reconciliation.* The last time I checked, there were no perfect

people on this planet. Periodically, I will invite the perfect people in our church to stand, and thus far we have found none. We are all fallen people, not just in principle but also in practice. James 3:2 reminds us that "we all stumble in many ways." You and I are in fact flawed. And if you are flawed, then those who live most closely with you know your flaws the best. Yet when was the last time you said to the people in your family, "I'm sorry. I was wrong. Please forgive me"? If we are failing and not saying those words, then we are failing big-time.

3. *Words of vision.* When we speak words of vision over our children, we paint a picture of effectiveness regarding their lives. "You're going to do something great with your life." "God's going to use your life in a cool way." "You're going to make a difference in this world." "You're going to be a godly woman." Words of vision build hope and confidence, and they are a vital part of the blessing.

4. *Words of security.* When my kids were growing up, I used to ask them almost every day, "How long will you be mine?" They would quickly respond, "Forever!" It was our little game, but it signified something very important. We need to say little things that imprint upon our children's hearts a sense of who God has created them to be.

The problem in our day, of course, is that spoken words take time. Mom tries to rush a few words in the bridal room while the photographer is there—but it's too late. All those things she wanted to say to her precious daughter, but now the years are gone, and with them the opportunity to communicate the blessing. Dad tries to slip a few words in just before his son jumps in the car and leaves for college. He can't believe that the days have slipped away, and he aches about all the things that he wanted to communicate—but never did.

I praise God for a father and a mother who understood this. I hope you'll permit me to share some personal illustrations to show the power that this truth has had in my own life. Here's a letter that my dad wrote to me on August 9, 1974. He was just thirty-eight years old, and though he still had some growing to do in "how to bless your children," you can see that the seeds were there. *"I guess this is the first time I have ever written you such a letter. We all miss you and are looking forward to having you home next week. It will be good to get our whole family under one roof again."*

The substance of the letter is generic stuff like, *"I fixed the garage. The roof is finished. Everything is cleaned up at home. The tomatoes are growing in the garden."* He didn't know what to say. But still, in his own way, he got this out at the end: *"Try to make the most of your last few days at camp. Both your mother and I are praying that this summer will have an important impact on your Christian life. Expecting to see you soon, Dad."*

Those who know my father could tell you that he now communicates love in far more eloquent terms than those, and that he has done so to all of his children many times over. I share that letter to encourage you. Even if you find loving words hard to come by, and even harder to express, you can start small, as he did, and allow God to grow your capacity to verbalize the blessing.

Compare the above to a blessing my dad wrote many years later, and you will begin to see just how much a person can grow. It's a note he wrote to my wife, Kathy, on the day that we got married. *"Dear Kathy, I don't write many letters, but somehow I felt constrained to drop you a line of encouragement today."* He goes on to exhort her in specific detail about some trials that were going on in our lives at the time of our marriage. But then he says these excellent words at the end of his letter: *"God will bring you through all of this, Kathy, when you commit each day to Him and trust Him to work things out."* And then he closes with these words of blessing: *"I commend to you my son. I love him dearly. I'll miss him deeply. But I give him up gladly to you since you are the one I have prayed for since his childhood that God would provide for him a virtuous woman. Her worth? 'Far above jewels' (Proverbs 31:10). You're it, Kathy. God bless you both. He has great things in store for you."*

Even now I am choked up as I reflect upon what those words have meant and do mean to me. I am reminded how desperately my children need to hear them. God forgive us for our silence when our words could make such a difference. Proverbs 3:27 says, **"Do not withhold good from those to whom it is due, when it is in your power to do it."** That's the blessing.

3. AFFIRMING YOUR CHILD'S VALUE

Let's go back to Isaac's blessing of Jacob in Genesis 27:27, **"So he came close and kissed him; and when he smelled the smell of his garments, he blessed him and said, 'See, the smell of my son is like the smell of a field which the Lord has blessed.'"** At the heart of the parental blessing is a word picture that communicates, "You matter to us," "We care about you," "You are special and unique." Affirming value is critical to a developing child's identity.

It's hard for me to believe that Isaac actually walked up to his forty-year-old son and smelled him, but that's what God's Word says. Can you imagine that? Isaac, by now an old man, comes close to Jacob—Esau, as far as he knows—and hugs him tightly and is like, "Boy, you are smelling *so* good today!" **"The smell of my son is like the smell of a field which the Lord has blessed."** It's a picture. It's as if Isaac is saying, "Do you know what I think of, Son, when I think of you? I see this field with grain growing. I hear the birds singing, and I see the sun shining. And you're in the middle of the field, tall and strong." He is communicating a powerful message to his son.

When my kids were very small, I picked some nicknames for each of them. (I'm not allowed to share those with you—they stay inside our house!) I also chose two words for each of our kids that Kathy and I would say to them over and over again. They were unique word pictures that were intended to affirm value. For example, the two words that we chose for Landon (who is fourteen now and reluctantly granted me permission to include this in the book) were "weird" and "wonderful." Those were our two words. He would come up and say, "What am I, Dad?" I would say, "You are weird and wonderful, Landon." Now you might think that *weird* is weird, but in our family *weird* isn't weird; *weird* is unique, different, not like anyone else, special, and precious.

So we would say, "Landon, what are you?" He'd be like, "I'm weird and wonderful!" And do you know what? He is! Special words are a powerful way to communicate love and affirmation and blessing to our children.

It seems like such a long time ago now, but I remember when my oldest son, Luke, was maybe four years old, and he was in the children's ministry in our church. He was coloring a picture, and apparently he got a little frustrated because he couldn't get it all inside the lines just right. Luke got so upset that he scribbled all over the paper. Well, there was one lady in our children's ministry back then who was a little difficult. She was pretty stiff and demanding and didn't seem to know how to jibe with the kids in a way that made them comfortable. When she saw the work Luke had done, she came by his little table to scold him.

"How could you do that? Look what you've done! That's not what I asked you to do! Your father is the pastor, and he wouldn't be very happy with you if he could see what you've just done!"

Without hesitation, Luke looked up at her and said, "My father loves *every-thing* I do."

Is that perfect or what? The funny thing is that he wasn't exactly correct, but I'm so glad he had a sense in his heart that, "I don't need your take on my dad's opinion of me. I may be four years old, but I *know* what he thinks of me!" All of us as parents must be certain that we do not fail to communicate this message of blessing to our kids.

I read recently of some parents who, every Christmas Eve after their children were in bed, would put some additional presents under the tree—one for each of their children. Written on each present was, "To Mom and Dad, From Jesus." On Christmas morning, the parents would go through a little ritual: "Oh, what's this? Wow, look! You kids aren't the only ones who are getting presents today. We got some, too, and they're from Jesus! You open them. We're just too excited to look. What do you think Jesus gave us?" Each child would open up the gift from Jesus and inside they would discover a picture of themselves.

The parents would say, "That's what we get again this year. God gave us *you!*" Of course, the first year it was a surprise and maybe the second year—but then to do this year after year after year. What an incredible picture of blessing to communicate to your children! Isn't that fantastic?

4. Spiritual Vision

Notice what Isaac said to Jacob in Genesis 27:28 as he blessed him: "**Now may God give you of the dew of heaven, and of the fatness of the earth, and an abundance of grain and new wine.**" Make no mistake—this wasn't a prayer for dew from heaven. Dew always comes from heaven. This was also not a prayer for grain, per se. No, this was a prayer for his son to connect the blessings of life with God: "May *God* give you these things."

What Isaac was doing was teaching his son to recognize that "**every good and perfect gift is from above**" (James 1:17 NIV). The blessings of life are from God. In every recorded blessing in the Old Testament, the child's relationship with God is prominent. Therefore, the blessing must include a spiritual vision.

Our children cannot make it without God. God help us if our primary vision for our kids is educational, athletic, or social, instead of spiritual. Just this week my kids were hassling me at home about "Why don't we get to do some of the things that other kids get to do?" I gathered them together for a big family conference and said, "Here's why: Because your mom and I are believing God for some fantastic kingdom purposes to be accomplished through you! You weren't born into this world just to mark time and flip a few pages on the calendar. God formed you in your mother's womb and gave you gifts and abilities that must be put to use for Him. The time is short. You can make a difference in this world. God wants to use your life."

Over the years, our church has formed a close partnership with a mission organization called Pioneers. Pioneers was started by a wonderful man named Ted Fletcher.[6] Ted understood the value of casting a spiritual vision for his children. Here's how he communicated it to his son, John. You may remember that in regard to John the Baptist, Scripture says, **"There was a man sent from God, whose name was John"** (John 1:6 NKJV). Growing up in the Fletcher home, John recalls, "Countless times, since I was a very small child, I remember my father saying to me, 'There was a man sent from God, whose name was John.'"

At age five, when young John was playing, his father would grab him and look into his eyes and say, "There was a man sent from God, whose name was John." In elementary school, John would come home and say, "Dad, how do I sort this out? What do I do?" Ted would remind his son, "There was a man sent from God, whose name was John." All through John's teen years and beyond, Ted was writing a spiritual vision on his heart.

I know that some parents make a huge deal about putting their kids to bed at night. I've done that quite a bit, but what I have done far more often is slipped into their rooms after they were asleep and knelt down beside their beds and prayed that God would use their lives to bring glory to Himself. Listen, parents: We need to be pouring a spiritual vision into our children. We don't want them to just get by; we want them to be the super conquerors that Christ Jesus has created them to be. A spiritual vision. "You are going to walk with God. You are going to love Him. You're going to be a godly man. You're going to be a woman of virtue and righteousness. And God is going to use your life."

5. Prosperous Vision

Here is Isaac's vision of prosperity for his son:

"Now may God give you of the dew of heaven, and of the fatness of the earth, and an abundance of grain and new wine; may peoples serve you, and nations bow down to you; be master of your brothers, and may your mother's sons bow down to you. Cursed be those who curse you, and blessed be those who bless you." (Genesis 27:28–29)

It is not biblical to pray for our kids to be wealthy. If they live in North America, then by global standards they are already wealthy, so don't worry about it. But, by the same token, it is not biblical to seek poverty for our children either. We need to pray that our kids will be prosperous in this world, that they will rise up and be successful by kingdom standards and be stewards of what they have for Christ's kingdom.

I think the key word in verse 29 is "master." Pray that your kids will master the opposition, master their roles in life, and master their finances—and not the reverse. That's what it means to cast a prosperous vision for our kids. It's not that the hardships and hassles and temptations of this world will not matter to them, but they will end up on top of all that, praising and thanking the God who made it possible.

WHAT HAPPENS WHEN THE BLESSING IS WITHHELD?

Perhaps you're reading this and saying to yourself, "I didn't get this when I was a kid." I know many people feel that way. When parents withhold the blessing from their children, either through ignorance or selfishness, the children will be tempted to respond in several ways that can actually make matters worse.

Some people try to earn the blessing. This leads to workaholism and other destructive pursuits of approval. It's like chasing a carrot on a stick. "Maybe if I do this, Dad will think I'm great." "Maybe if I achieve this." "Maybe if I reach this goal." How many times I have watched a man woo and win a woman, only to quickly set her aside and go right back to pursuing the approval of his parents! When the blessing is withheld, some people try to earn it.

Some people search for the blessing elsewhere. They pull back from their parents and move away. Some may even get violent. Many studies indicate that the number one candidate for gangs and cults is a kid who did not receive the blessing from his or her parents. Recently, I was talking with an inner-city pastor about this very issue. He told me, "James, you could walk down any street where I minister and line ten men up against a wall and ask, 'Did you receive the blessing from your parents?' Again and again you would hear, 'No.' 'No.' 'No.' 'No.' 'No.' 'No.'" I wonder how much of the criminal, pernicious behavior observed in young adults is traceable back to absent fathers and homes without the blessing.

Some people withdraw into a world of isolation and loneliness. They just pull back and shut down. It's almost as if their world comes to an end. Having been hurt by those from whom they most needed to receive love, they conclude that being alone is better than making oneself vulnerable to others and then being wounded when they don't come through.

Some people strike out in anger. This is the worst response. Have you ever considered the degree to which high school and young adult aggression is just the surfacing anger of parental neglect? Parents ask their kids, "Why are you acting like this? Why are you causing us so much grief? Why are you refusing to live under our rules and participate in family life? What happened to you?" Very few teens understand their own feelings well enough to truly answer those kind of questions, but if they could you might hear, "Because I can't stand another day of seeking and failing to receive your approval. Because I find more love and affection in my peer group than I ever receive at home. Because winning your attention through disobedience is better than winning your apathy and distractedness by being a 'good kid.'" Sad but true, many parents understand the transforming power of giving the blessing only when the damage of not offering it to their kids has already been done.

When the blessing is given, a child emerges into adulthood able to answer the three most important questions in life:

1. Who am I? (a question of identity)
2. Why am I here? (a question of security)
3. Where am I going? (a question of confidence)

If you have received the blessing, you probably have a very good handle on those three things: Who am I? Why am I here? Where am I going? With those questions answered, life can be very fulfilling and fruitful, but without them, an enormous amount of energy is diverted into all sorts of futile searches for the blessing. As the song says, "Looking for love in all the wrong places."

HOW DO YOU LIVE
WITHOUT THE BLESSING?

Maybe you are reading this and are having a hard time relating the truths to your children, because your mind keeps drifting to the fact that you did not receive the blessing from your parents and that missing the blessing has affected you negatively. Maybe you are wondering how people are supposed to live without the blessing and then give it to their kids—regardless of their own experience. In that respect, let me suggest two things that, if diligently pursued, will bring incredible results in your own life.

HEARING YOUR SPIRITUAL LEADERS

I believe that hearing your spiritual leaders is a key purpose of the local church. We, as God's servants, can communicate to the Lord's people those things that perhaps their own family never said to them. The church is your family, and we can get this message through to one another—together.

The Bible tells us that Timothy grew up without a father. He was raised by his mother, Eunice, and his grandmother, Lois. Timothy didn't have a father, but do you know what he did have? He made out pretty well—he had the apostle Paul. Paul wasn't his physical father, but he became like a father. Listen to some of his words: **"Timothy, my true child in the faith"** (1 Timothy 1:2); **"Timothy, my son"** (1 Timothy 1:18); **"Timothy, my beloved son"** (2 Timothy 1:2). Paul told Timothy, **"Let no one look down on your youthfulness"** and **"Do not neglect the spiritual gift within you"** (1 Timothy 4:12, 14). Such words appear throughout Paul's two letters to Timothy. All of that is an illustration of this truth: God can provide spiritual leaders—spiritual fathers and mothers—to pick up the slack left by our earthly parents. Those of you who are mature in the Lord and have already received the blessing have a responsibility to share it with others. It's not just about your own children.

HEARING YOUR HEAVENLY FATHER

We need to affirm one another to the best of our ability, but of course we will never be everything that we should be for each other. That's why it's also important to hear our heavenly Father. It is possible that Jesus never received the blessing from Joseph, his own earthly father. Normally, if a child were born of uncertain parentage, he or she would not receive the formal ceremony of blessing that we talked about earlier. Because of the questions surrounding the child's birth, the father would be reticent to invite his friends to come. Since Joseph was a righteous man (Matthew 1:19), it is doubtful that he would have withheld his blessing for this reason. More likely, Joseph died before he was able to bestow it upon Jesus.

How significant, then, were the words spoken during Jesus' baptism? Matthew 3:16–17 tells us that the heavens were opened and the Spirit of God descended in the form of a dove. And a voice came from heaven saying, **"This is My beloved Son, in whom I am well-pleased."** Isn't that great? God the Father Himself modeled the importance of affirmation.

Here is the good news. If you have turned from your sin and embraced Christ by faith, then you are the son or the daughter of almighty God. At the end of the day, it doesn't really matter what your earthly father says about you, or what your mother doesn't say. What really matters is what God says about you. He loves you and wants to minister to you.

Will you receive this word from your heavenly Father, "This is My beloved son, in whom I am well-pleased." Or, "This is My beloved daughter, in whom I am well-pleased." Allow God to speak that truth into your life. It's a message we need to hear again and again.

A PRAYER TO GO HIGHER

→ ←

Lord, thank You for loving me and affirming me as Your child. I so need that in my life! Thank You for being such a tender Father. Help me to please You and bring glory to Your name by living in light of Your blessing, regardless of whether or not I received it from my own parents. Grant me a spirit of forgiveness toward my mom and dad for any failure on their part to pass along the blessing.

Lord, I want to chart a course that pleases You with the children in my own life. Help me to take any and every opportunity to convey the blessing to them. May they come to understand that You have a unique vision for their lives. Help me to give this blessing to those I love. I pray this in the strong name of Jesus. Amen.

A PROJECT TO GO DEEPER

→→ ←←

From the example of Isaac blessing Jacob in Genesis 27, we learned five important steps for communicating the blessing to our children: *meaningful touch, spoken words, affirming value, spiritual vision, and prosperous vision.* In Genesis 48:9–16, we encounter Jacob (or Israel) blessing two of his grandsons, Ephraim and Manasseh. Read through that passage several times and see if you can identify the same five steps for conveying the blessing.

A PRACTICE TO GO FURTHER

→→ ←←

It's time to evaluate how well you're doing at communicating the blessing to the kids in your life. Take out a piece of paper, and make a chart. (You can also use the form shown in appendix A.) Across the top, assign a column for each of the five steps in the blessing mentioned above. Along the side, designate a row for each child who is a regular part of your life. These could be your own children, nieces or nephews, younger cousins, kids you teach in the children's program at church, neighborhood kids, etc. Reflect upon your interactions with each of them. How are you doing at conveying the blessing to each child? What can you do to communicate the blessing with greater purpose in each of the five ways?

NOTES

1. For much of this chapter, I am indebted to ideas contained in Gary Smalley and John Trent's *The Blessing* (Nashville: Nelson, 1986).
2. "Alumni Association News," *UCLA Monthly,* March–April 1981, as cited in Smalley and Trent, *The Blessing,* 46.
3. Smalley and Trent, *The Blessing,* 47.
4. Helen Colton, *The Gift of Touch* (New York: Seavien/Putnam, 1983), 102; as cited in Smalley and Trent, *The Blessing,* 48.
5. Ross Campbell, *How to Really Love Your Child* (Wheaton, Ill.: Victor, 1977), 73; as cited in Smalley and Trent, *The Blessing,* 49.
6. See Ted Fletcher, *When God Comes Calling* (Mobile, Ala.: Gazette Press, 2001).

WORD #3:
HONOR

→>- -<-

Long before David Letterman was making Top Ten lists, God had His own Top Ten list. Recorded in Exodus 20, you might know it by its more common name: the Ten Commandments. Do you remember the background? The children of Israel are making their journey from Egypt to the Promised Land. Three months into the trip, Moses heads up Mount Sinai to meet with God and soon returns with these stone tablets. On them are written God's top-ten, bottom-line-you-better-get-this-stuff-done commandments.

Exodus 20:1–2 says, **"Then God spoke all these words, saying, 'I am the Lord your God, who brought you out of the land of Egypt, out of the house of slavery.'"** Then come the commandments:

1. **"You shall have no other gods before Me."** (verse 3)
2. **"You shall not make for yourself an idol."** (verse 4)
3. **"You shall not take the name of the Lord your God in vain."** (verse 7)
4. **"Remember the sabbath day, to keep it holy."** (verse 8)

And then, number 5 on God's Top Ten list: **"Honor your father and your mother, that your days may be prolonged in the land which the Lord your God gives you"** (verse 12).

There it is—*honor*. Honor is the third word to change your family. You may be surprised to find that honor is a very important concept in Scripture. In Deuteronomy 5:16, the fifth commandment is repeated (with an expanded blessing): "**Honor your father and your mother, as the Lord your God has commanded you, that your days may be prolonged and that it may go well with you on the land which the Lord your God gives you.**"

Now you may say, "Well, that's just the Old Testament." But wait. So significant was this that the apostle Paul, under the inspiration of the Spirit of God, repeated the command in his letter to the Ephesians: "**Honor your father and mother (which is the first commandment with a promise), so that it may be well with you, and that you may live long on the earth**" (6:2–3). Clearly, this is a command for all people in all periods of history.

A UNIVERSAL COMMAND

When I say *all*, I mean small children to middle-aged adults to older adults. If you have parents, you are to honor them no matter how old you may be. We never outgrow this command. It is for every race, for every nation, for every culture—even in North America, where the idea of honoring parents is typically ridiculed. In our day, we place a lot higher premium upon honoring *self* at the expense of those around us who need and deserve to be honored. But we must remember that this is a commandment. Regardless of your parents' success rating, regardless of how you may feel about it, God commands all of His people everywhere, "Honor your father and mother."

The Hebrew term for *honor* means literally "a heavy weight" or "to lay it on them." Now in our society, "laying it on" is a term of insincerity. "Boy, she really laid it on!" Or, "Man, he was really spreading it thick!" However, honoring our parents is an action of deep sincerity. Far more than surface flattery, biblical honor involves locating the things that your parents have done right and then praising them for those things—whatever they might be.

You say, "OK, I see that honoring my parents is in God's Top Ten. No doubt about it. But why is this such a big deal?" Here's why: When children do not honor their parents, the very fabric of society begins to unravel. It was the ancient Greek philosopher, Plato, who said, "What is honored in a land will be cultivated there."

WHAT IF MY PARENTS
DID A LOUSY JOB?

In his excellent book *The Tribute and the Promise,* Dennis Rainey wrote:

Honoring your parents is an attitude accompanied by actions that says to your parents: "You are worthy. You have value. You are the person God sovereignly placed in my life. You may have failed me, hurt me, and disappointed me at times, but I am taking off my judicial robe and releasing you from the courtroom of my mind. I choose to look at you with compassion—as people with needs, concerns, and scars of your own."[1]

All children are commanded to honor their parents—even if the parents did a lousy job.

In the Old Testament Law, God reveals His heart toward people who don't honor their parents. This is serious stuff. For example, **"He who strikes his father or his mother shall surely be put to death"**; and **"He who curses his father or his mother shall surely be put to death"** (Exodus 21:15, 17).

Truth be told, I said some things to my parents in my foolish high school years that I greatly regret. Maybe you have, too. I am so glad that we don't live in the Old Testament time period, or some of us wouldn't be here. But that is still God's heart. That's how God feels about anyone who would make the choice to dishonor his or her parents. It's extremely serious!

IF YOU KNEW MY PARENTS,
YOU'D KNOW THIS IS IMPOSSIBLE!

You may be saying, "Man, if you think for a moment that I am going to do *anything* to encourage my old man—you must be crazy!" But wait. I want to be really clear because I know that some people have hurtful relationships with their parents.

Honoring your parents does not mean these three things:

1. Honoring your parents does not mean *groveling and seeking their approval.* God wants us to be free from bondage to anyone's approval but

His. The apostle Paul said, **"If I were still trying to please men, I would not be a bond-servant of Christ"** (Galatians 1:10).

2. Honoring your parents does not mean *making yourself vulnerable to their hurtful behavior*. Grown children can choose appropriate boundaries between themselves and their parents.

3. Honoring your parents does not mean *ignoring or denying the past*. God's purposes are not advanced when we act as though certain issues do not exist. But forgiveness demands that those issues not influence your attitude toward your parents.

However, honoring your parents *does* mean:

1. Honoring your parents means *choosing to place great value on your relationship with them* and knocking off the attitude that "it doesn't matter." Listen, it *does* matter. It matters to God, and it should matter to you.

2. Honoring your parents means *taking the initiative to improve the relationship* in whatever increments you can.

3. Honoring your parents means *recognizing that they have done some things right*. You might be thinking, *My parents didn't do* anything *right!* Your perspective is clouded, perhaps by great pain. But they did *something* right. If you open your heart to this truth, God will show you.

4. Honoring your parents means *acknowledging the sacrifices they have made for you*.

5. Honoring your parents means *seeing them as Christ does*, with compassion and mercy.

6. Honoring your parents means *forgiving them*, even as God in Christ has forgiven you.

WHEN WE HONOR OUR PARENTS, IT BLESSES US.

Perhaps you're wondering, "And why would I do this?" Very simple: When we honor our parents, it blesses us.

That's good news, isn't it? Now don't think that's a cheesy motivation just because it's a benefit to you. Some people think it's wrong to obey God for their own benefit. Not so! If it were wrong, God would not have written the benefits of obedience into Scripture. On the contrary, God often motivates His children by promising to bless them. Remember that Ephesians 6:2 says, "**Honor your father and mother (which is the first commandment with a promise).** If you recall back in Exodus 20, God gave the first four commandments, and He presented no reason or rationale for any of them. It's just like, "Do it! I am God, and you are not! So do it!" But then in the fifth commandment, things changed—"**that your days may be prolonged**" (verse 12), or as Paul put it: "**That it may be well with you, and that you may live long on the earth**" (Ephesians 6:3).

If God goes out of His way to record for us the benefits of obeying a certain command, it is not wrong to desire those benefits. In fact, doesn't every decision of obedience bring blessing? God uses that to encourage us to live for Him.

What's the Blessing?

Let's look at the benefits of honoring our parents more closely: "**that it may be well with you.**" What kind of promise is this? Is it health? Is it wealth? Is it safety? Is it an easier life? Is it relational favor with God? All I can tell you is this: I don't know exactly what it means. I don't know what the blessings are that come from choosing to honor your parents. But the Bible says good things are going to happen. How often I have people come and say to me, "I have been seeking God and praying about this one thing, but I just don't seem to get an answer. Why isn't God—?" I'll tell you what. Get everything done that God has asked you to do, and then just see if God doesn't meet your needs in some phenomenal way. I don't know how it is that God will bless you. It could be that God will bless you at your point of greatest need if you obey the command to honor your parents.

How to Live Long

Here's the second blessing phrase: "**that you may live long on the earth.**" That's more specific, isn't it? The first and most obvious meaning of this phrase is that those who honor their parents will live longer than those who don't. The medical studies I mentioned in chapter 2 confirm that people who off-load bitterness, negativity, and unforgiveness experience better health. If you choose to sin, you choose to suffer. God's Word is very clear about that, so it shouldn't surprise us that a person who pursues obedience at every level is healthier, happier, and lives longer.

But if we look a little deeper, I think God is promising even more than a longer life for the one who chooses to obey. I believe "that you may live long on the earth" is also making a promise about your legacy. In the family that chooses to honor the parents, there is a ripple effect that goes on for many years. When I honor my parents, my kids see something modeled; they will likely then choose to honor me, and through them the blessing of my obedience can continue into the third and fourth generations.

You say, "Well, I don't think my parents honored their parents." Drive a stake in the ground right now. Maybe they didn't know what you know. Just say, "As for *my* family, in the future, things are going to be different." If you honor your parents, your kids will notice, and then turn the calendar a few more pages to their kids and their kids' kids—the influence of your life can continue for many generations.

WHEN WE DON'T HONOR OUR PARENTS, IT DEVASTATES THEM.

You say, "My parents don't care. They don't give a rip about what I say to them." You couldn't be more wrong! I want us to look again at the story of David and Absalom (2 Samuel 18–19) that we touched on briefly in chapter 1. It illustrates so vividly that when we don't honor our parents, it devastates them.

THE STORY OF DAVID AND ABSALOM

When Absalom killed his half-brother as revenge for the rape of his sister, Tamar, the family began to break down pretty rapidly. David was so angry with Absalom that he fled the city of Jerusalem to avoid his father's wrath. In fact, Absalom spent three whole years in exile and had no contact of any kind with his father. Given these circumstances, wouldn't you think that David would be filled with rage and hatred toward his son during this time of banishment? Yet look at 2 Samuel 13:39, **"The heart of King David longed to go out to Absalom."** I'm thinking, "Dude, you're the king! If you want to go *be* with Absalom, go *be* with him!" But David was like, "I *want* to be with him, but I am so angry at him." David hated his son's actions, but still there remained that deep love that exists between members of the same family.

Maybe a similar situation exists in your family this very moment. Maybe you have been "banished" by your parents and wrongly assume that they also do not love you.

David finally overcame his negative feelings enough to call for his son to come home. Picture the scene. As soon as Absalom gets back to Jerusalem, you would expect some big party, right? Wrong! **"Now Absalom lived two full years in Jerusalem, and did not see the king's face"** (2 Samuel 14:28). When Absalom does make it back to Jerusalem, David refuses to see him.

The king's son is living right in the same city, and he doesn't see his own father for two more years! Frustrated, Absalom says, **"Why have I come from Geshur? It would be better for me still to be there. Now therefore, let me see the king's face"** (verse 32). This is such a vivid illustration of the mixed messages we often send in our own families.

Finally, David allows Absalom to come in: **"Thus he came to the king and prostrated himself on his face to the ground before the king, and the king kissed Absalom"** (verse 33).

MORE TROUBLE AHEAD

You might think that from here on everything was headed in a good direction in this father/son relationship. Not so! Second Samuel 15 tells us that Absalom went out and stirred up trouble. Apparently, on a daily basis men from all over the nation of Israel would journey to the palace to ask King David for his advice. Absalom began intercepting these people and saying, "Forget about what my dad says! I'm the guy who knows what's up. You ought to be talking to me!" In fact, 2 Samuel 15:6 says, **"In this manner Absalom dealt with all Israel who came to the king for judgment; so Absalom stole away the hearts of the men of Israel."**

According to verse 12, **"And the conspiracy was strong, for the people increased continually with Absalom."** This is conspiracy of the worst kind. The son, rejected for five years but now reconciled to his father, still has so much anger in his heart that he pulled the nation away from his dad. It became so bad for King David that he actually had to flee the city of Jerusalem.

David is devastated by Absalom and this group of conspirators: "**David went up the ascent of the Mount of Olives, and wept as he went, and his head was covered and he walked barefoot. Then all the people who were with him each covered his head and went up weeping as they went**" (2 Samuel 15:30).

Once David is outside the city, some members of his army come to him and say, "We are going to take the kingdom back. We are going to defeat your son, Absalom. We can win this! We can get the throne back for you, David." So David said, "OK, go get the throne back and win the battle, but don't hurt Absalom."

"Don't worry," they said. "We won't *hurt* him—we're going to *kill* him!"

"Don't you dare!" David answered, and he threatened them and anyone who would touch him.

"*What* are you talking about? This treacherous so-called son of yours— why are you being so protective?"

David's only answer was "Don't hurt him. Don't hurt him" (see 2 Samuel 18:1–5).

So what happens? Well, the battle is fought, and Absalom *is* killed. When a messenger arrives with news from the battle, the first words out of David's mouth are, "**Is it well with the young man Absalom?**" (2 Samuel 18:29). All David cares about is whether his son is OK. The guy is like, "You know, I am not even going to answer that!" Soon a second messenger appears. Again, the first question out of David's mouth is, "**Is it well with the young man Absalom?**" (verse 32). Out comes the news that Absalom is dead.

David was devastated again.

> The king was deeply moved and went up to the chamber over the gate and wept. And thus he said as he walked, "O my son Absalom, my son, my son Absalom! Would I had died instead of you, O Absalom, my son, my son!" (verse 33)

You see all of this happening and you think, *David, are you crazy? This is the son you wouldn't even talk to for five years! Remember, he stole the kingdom from you! And now you are so brokenhearted?* Second Samuel 19 tells us the king continued to grieve: "**Behold, the king is weeping and mourns for Absalom**" (verse 1). "**The king is grieved for his son**" (verse 2). "**The king covered his face and cried out with a loud voice, 'O my son Absalom, O Absalom, my son, my son!'**" (verse 4).

So bizarre is this love/hate scene that Joab, the former commander of David's army, says in 2 Samuel 19:5–6,

> "Today you have covered with shame the faces of all your servants, who today have saved your life and the lives of your sons and daughters, the lives of your wives, and the lives of your concubines, by loving those who hate you, and by hating those who love you. For you have shown today that princes and servants are nothing to you; for I know this day that if Absalom were alive and all of us were dead today, then you would be pleased."

Is that unbelievable? Joab says, "You are messed up so bad! We went out to get the whole kingdom back for you, and you are more upset about your one son who died than all of the people who died (and could have died) in seeking to win the kingdom back for you!"

An Unbreakable Bond

Here is the point. The relationship between a father and a son, between a mother and daughter, is so powerful that no negative circumstance can ever break that bond. Perhaps you have had an awful relationship with your parents. Or maybe it was good early in your life, but now that you are grown and married you have drifted far apart. You're thinking to yourself, *My parents never think about me!* You're wrong. They are thinking of you *right now.* You may say, "Well, why don't they call me?" Because in some ways your relationship with your parents is like the one David had with Absalom. There is a very strong mixture of love and frustration that causes people to act in ways that may be very different from what they truly feel. If that cycle is to be broken, *someone* has to go first.

I am challenging you, as a follower of Jesus Christ, to step up to the plate. Maybe you find yourself in a situation not unlike Absalom, where all the signals from your parents seem to say, "Stay away! We don't need your honor!"

Don't believe it! Just as there is within the heart of every child a longing for the blessing, so there is within the heart of every parent a longing to be honored and recognized for the love that has been given.

No More Childish Behavior

I tell you with great certainty that your parents *do* care, and it *does* matter to them. You say, "You don't know my parents. You don't know what they've done and not done. There's no way that I'm going to honor them." Look with me at 1 Corinthians 13, a great portion of Scripture often read at weddings. It's about love, but it includes an important truth in verse 11: **"When I was a child, I used to speak like a child, think like a child, reason like a child; when I became a man, I did away with childish things."**

How do children **speak?** "Give me what I want! Why can't I? That's not fair! When is it my turn? I need more of that! Wah, wah, wah, wah!" And how do they **think?** *Why are we doing that? I don't like that. Let's do what I like to do. Why do we always have to do what she wants?* Everything revolves around them. And how do they **reason?** *How can I get another cookie? I wonder what I'll get for my birthday next year. It's only three-hundred-sixty-four days away.* Isn't that how a child reasons?

"When I was a child, I used to speak like a child, think like a child, reason like a child; when I became a man, I did away with childish things"— well, at least I was *supposed* to do away with childish things. Putting away childish things includes learning to see my parents from an adult's perspective, not from a child's perspective.

TRAGICALLY, SOME GROWNUPS CONTINUE TO ACT LIKE CHILDREN TOWARD THEIR OWN PARENTS.

Those grown-ups mature in their relations and dealings with others, but when they get with their mom and dad, they're like little kids again. "How come you didn't call me?" and, "You promised to do this," and, "You said you would," and, "That's not what I asked you for!" Erma Bombeck once wrote that children never seem to figure out that their parents also have expectations and that they need something in return for their love. We are so slow to figure out that our parents are "vulnerable human beings who can also be hurt," Bombeck noted.

Deep within every parent's heart—whether he or she can articulate it or not—is a longing for the day when one's precious child comes around the corner and says, "You really *did* love me. And some of those things that you told me to do that I thought were so bizarre—I was wrong and you were right! And when I was an immature student who thought I had all the answers and made things so hard for you—I knew nothing! I am so sorry for all the grief that I gave you. You didn't do everything perfectly, but you were a good dad! You were a good mom!"

Those are adult words, mature words. They recognize the parent's love and give true honor.

IT'S TIME TO HONOR OUR PARENTS.

Clearly, this is something that God Himself wants communicated. It is time to honor our parents . . .

1. Even if we don't feel like it.

That is part of becoming adults, isn't it? It is doing some things we don't feel like doing. Do you ever do things you don't feel like doing? Do you ever read your Bible when you don't feel like doing it? Good decision. A couple of mornings this week, I didn't feel like going to work. Guess what? I went anyway. We do lots of things we don't feel like doing. God forgive us for being so selfish and childish regarding our own parents! How many times have our moms and dads done things they didn't feel like doing?

Maybe you feel angry or hurt or neglected or misunderstood by your parents. It's time to get past those things. As children, we must honor our parents because raising kids is an exhausting process, because kids often bring a lot of pain into their parents' lives that we fail to see, and because *our* kids will soon grow up to treat us the way we treated our parents. Don't miss that point. Your kids will grow up and handle you in your later years the way they have observed you treat your own parents.

When we de-prioritize our parents as though our lives were more important, when we communicate to our parents through word or deed that they do not hold a place of honor in our lives and schedules, we have committed a great sin. First Timothy 5:8 says, **"If anyone does not provide for his own, and especially for those of his household, he has denied the faith and is worse**

than an unbeliever." That provision is to be far more than simply financial. It should involve the giving of our time and emotional energy also.

I once came across the following letter:

> When my husband died ten years ago, that was a shock. But an even greater shock has been the reaction of my four grown children. There was no hope of getting my husband back, but I was hoping at least to have a good relationship with my children. I don't require that much from my daughter and sons—just a bit of communication, just a phone call. But I could go for six weeks at a time and never hear from a member of my family. Four children, eight grandchildren. Not a phone call.
>
> I noticed that when they do call, it is always for some reason. It is never, "Mother, are you alright?" I have Parkinson's disease, and I am diabetic. It's not that they don't know I am under different kinds of treatment, but they never want to hear anything about it. I think it's because they don't want to be responsible for me. I really can't think of another reason why they wouldn't call.
>
> I called my son at his office last fall to tell him something funny that had happened. I started the conversation by saying, "Well, I know you're busy, but I just wanted to call and hear your voice and see if you're OK." He responded, "Yes, I've been busy." So I said, "You know that old piece of property that your dad bought before he died?" He didn't answer me so I went on. "You know he bought it when it was outside the city. He paid just $500 for a one-acre lot. Well, the real estate agent came by. He said it is worth $12,000! Isn't that incredible?" He said, "Mother, you may live for five or ten more years. If you start selling everything you have, there won't be anything left to take care of you." I responded, "Honey, I have enough. I'll be fine—"
>
> His voice went tense. "Well, I want you to know that I can't work any harder, and I just can't take care of you." I said, "You won't have to. Please don't worry about that." I finally said, "Honey, I just called to hear your voice. And I have. I am going to hang up now."
>
> I can't share any of my joys. They are ignoring me, and my grandchildren, too. They have cars, but I don't see them. There are so many things about me they don't even know."[2]

This should not be true among the Lord's people. Failing to honor our parents is wrong, wrong, wrong! It is time to honor our parents, even if we don't feel like it.

2. Even if they won't receive it.

You may be thinking, *If I would try to honor my parents, they wouldn't hear me. I can already hear the door slamming or the phone clicking down.* That is what the Prodigal Son was thinking (Luke 15). He got his share of the family inheritance, then took off to live like a pig, and before long found himself living *with* the pigs. Do you remember that story? When he came to the end of his funds and the beginning of his senses, he decided, "I'm just going to live in the barn. I'll be my dad's slave." And as he made his way home, he was so nervous that his dad was going to reject him. But do you know what the Scriptures say? **"While he was still a long way off, his father saw him and felt compassion for him, and ran and embraced him and kissed him"** (Luke 15:20). How surprised he was!

You may be surprised how receptive your parents are. And besides, we don't do what we do for the response. We do it because we believe God's Word and want to obey Him. So it's time to honor our parents even if they won't receive it.

3. Even if they have been abusive

Maybe your parents have been emotionally, physically, or even sexually abusive—some of the most painful experiences a child can face. But note this:

1. Focusing on the pain only perpetuates it;
2. Finding something good to focus on promotes healing and reconciliation, as hard as that may be;
3. Honoring your parents does not mean exposing yourself to further pain. It is just a step of obedience to God that will yield good results in your life; and
4. Honoring your parents helps to break the chains of bitterness and unforgiveness.

Honoring our parents is something we do from day to day and year to year. It is reflected in every conversation we have and every hour we spend with our parents. Yet, if you have read my writings, you know that I believe in both a *crisis* and a *process* in all matters of transformation. The process of honoring our parents is done in a thousand little things over time, but the crisis is essential to jump-start that process. As a crisis for honoring your parents, I strongly recommend Dennis Rainey's idea of writing a formal tribute.[3]

GIVE A TRIBUTE TO YOUR PARENTS!

In this written tribute, you can acknowledge all the good that they have done for you. Tell them how thankful you are to be their son or daughter. Express your love for them and recognize their sacrifices on your behalf.

I wrote a tribute both to my mom and dad. (They are included in appendix B under "Sample Tributes.") Keep in mind that I've spent my whole life learning to write and speak. I don't want you to think, "*I* could never say it like that!" It doesn't matter how I say it; what matters is how *you* choose to honor your mom and dad.

My Big Surprise

I didn't think a written tribute would be that big of a deal to my parents. I have always had a great relationship with them, and I really didn't think they would find much impact in my tribute, already knowing how I felt. Wow, was I wrong! When I read my tribute to my mom in front of our whole family, she just cried and smiled. I knew from looking into her eyes that it meant more to her than I ever imagined. About two years later, my parents were down from Canada for Thanksgiving, and I did the same for my dad. He, too, was deeply touched, and I felt good about having made my obedience to God's Word "official," thinking that would be the last I heard of the crisis part.

If you can believe it, my mom took those two $8\frac{1}{2}$ x 11" written tributes of honor and framed them with a picture of herself and my dad in the middle, and hung it over her bed! Did it matter to her? It meant so much to her that she didn't ever want to forget it! Believe me, whether your relationship has been phenomenal or very difficult, God will use this step of obedience with your parents more than you can imagine. After all, it's one of His Top Ten: "**Honor your father and your mother**" (Exodus 20:12).

GETTING STARTED

Here are some practical ideas to get you started:

1. *Be honest.* Don't say a bunch of slobbery things you don't mean. You don't have to pretend that you approve of everything your parents do or that they are perfect. My parents were not perfect.
2. *Be positive.* Just focus on the good. Philippians 4:8 says, "**Whatever is true, whatever is honorable, whatever is right, whatever is pure, whatever is lovely, whatever is of good repute . . . dwell on these things.**" Focus on the good—whatever it is. If you can't see it, pray and ask the Lord for wisdom, and He will show it to you.
3. *Be public.* Do this in front of your spouse and children, if possible. It is a wonderful teaching moment. God will use it to spread a legacy of honor throughout your family.
4. *Be decisive.* Don't put it off. The time is now.

HONOR YOUR PARENTS ASAP!

Within a few weeks of preaching this message in our church, I received a letter from a man that powerfully underscores the need to get this done as soon as you can:

Dear Pastor James,

I really enjoyed the recent series that you taught us on words to change your family. The word I wish to point out is honor. Shortly before you presented that word, I had been feeling that I should spend more time with my parents. . . . So, on the weekend, I went over to my parents' house to spend some time with them and help them with house and yard work. Later that week, I took them out to dinner. I believe it was the first time I had ever treated them! While at dinner, I thanked them for being the parents that they were to me. On the following weekend, I spent a few more hours at their place working with my dad. My mom called the following day to thank me. I told her that it was a small way to say, "I love you." I spent the following weekend with them as well.

Not too long after that, my entire family got together at my brother's house for his birthday. We had a fabulous time being with one another! We even took a family picture. Little did I know that night would be the last time I would ever talk to my mom. Just a few days later, my brother called and said that Mom was not breathing and that the paramedics were giving her CPR. My wife and I rushed over to the hospital. We were waiting in the emergency room when they pulled her out of the ambulance and rushed her into a closed section of the emergency room. After about ten minutes, the doctor informed us that my mom had passed away. My mom had a severe asthma attack. She passed out, and the doctors think she had a heart attack. She always had problems with asthma, but they were never life-threatening.

So I want to thank you for the challenge that you presented in your message. I will forever cherish the memories that I had with my mom for the past couple of months. That picture we took at my brother's house ended up being the last that we had of her. I will now cherish all the time that I have with my dad and with other loved ones, and I will seek to honor them every chance that I have.

COMMON QUESTIONS

I want to close this chapter a little differently, addressing common questions about honoring our parents.

Question: I want to honor my parents, but what should I do if they are deceased? Have I forfeited my opportunity?
Answer: We are responsible for what we know, aren't we? Perhaps you had never heard about this or didn't understand it clearly until now. That's OK. Now you are responsible to do what you know. If your parents have already died, I would still encourage you to write some things down to the best of your ability and say in front of your family, "Here is some stuff I wish I had said to Mom. I didn't say it when she was here, but I now know from God's Word that I should have. I just want to acknowledge before my family that I was wrong. But I want to do it as best as I can." God will use that in your family.

Q: All of my brothers and sisters have accepted the Lord as Savior. Is it dishonoring to them if I just go ahead and do this on my own, or should I at least talk to them about it before I "beat them to the punch"?

A: The race is on! That's a great thing. In our family, probably by virtue of the career path I have chosen, I have taken the lead on things like this. Yet my siblings feel the same way about my parents. I would encourage you to talk to your brothers and/or sisters. Maybe the Lord will allow you to do this together. I don't think it is really clear in Scripture whether honor should be given corporately or separately. It would probably mean a great deal to your parents to hear from all of their children at one time. But at the end of the day, make sure that *you* get it done regardless of the willingness of your brothers or sisters.

Q: I have an absentee father. I don't know where he is or how to contact him. What should I do?

A: Start by writing out a tribute so that the things you want to say are ready to be said. Then I would begin to pray, "God, give me an opportunity to find out where my dad is. I want so much to say these things to him." Just leave that in God's hands. You might be surprised what the Lord will do when you desire to obey Him.

Q: My father doesn't want to see me or talk to me. In fact, things are so bad between us that I am to the point where it's like, "I don't even have a father." The only person that I consider my father is God. What should I do?

A: First of all, I think you need to circle back to chapter 2 and reread the stuff about forgiveness. It sounds like there is some follow-through in this matter of forgiveness that you still need to work on. I think the chapter will help you and be an encouragement to you.

I know what it means to be so hurt by your parents that you say, "I don't have a father. God is my Father." Certainly, God wants to fill up in your life what is lacking in regard to your father. But God does not want any of us to dishonor our parents. It will take a supernatural capacity for you to love your father in spite of the rejection you have experienced. But God wants to give you the capacity to love your father.

I would encourage you to step out by faith and write a tribute to your dad and put it in the mail. You can follow up later with a phone call. I guarantee you that, regardless of your dad's response, God will bless you.

A PRAYER TO GO HIGHER

Lord, I acknowledge that Your ways are always best. Please forgive me for failing to do what You clearly command in Your Word. I have not honored my parents to the best of my abilities. I have not been the child that I could have been—and should have been. Help me to honor my parents in a significant way through a formal, written tribute. Prepare their hearts to receive it, Lord. And strengthen me to honor them in small ways on a day-to-day basis. May I seize every opportunity to give them the respect they deserve.

Thank You, Lord, for Your promise that when I do this, You will bless me in ways that I can't even imagine. Grant me a long and prosperous life, Lord. May You receive all the glory that comes from my obedience to You. I pray this in Jesus' name, the name that is most worthy of honor. Amen.

A PROJECT TO GO DEEPER

Honor is a big deal to God! It's a theme that's present throughout the pages of Scripture. Even more important than His command that we honor our parents, however, is His righteous expectation that we honor *Him*. Take some time to look up the following passages and jot down what they teach you about honoring God: 1 Samuel 2:30; Psalm 50:15; Jeremiah 13:11; Malachi 2:2; John 5:23; 1 Corinthians 6:20; Hebrews 5:4; Revelation 4:11.

At a practical level, how can you improve at honoring God this week?

A PRACTICE TO GO FURTHER

This should be obvious by now. The entire chapter has pointed you toward the step of writing a formal tribute to each of your parents. You need to get this done! Use some of the suggestions I gave you earlier in the chapter, and feel free to look at the copies of my tributes to my own parents (which are in appendix B). But just be yourself, and tell them what's on your heart.

Once you've written the tributes, give some thought about how you will present them to your parents. This is perhaps as important as the actual words on the page. If possible, honor your mom and dad publicly, and allow your example to spur on other members of your family to do the same.

NOTES

1. Dennis Rainey with David Boehl, *The Tribute and the Promise* (Nashville: Nelson, 1994), 39.
2. Source unknown.
3. My thinking has been greatly influenced by the work of Dennis Rainey in his book, *The Tribute and the Promise*.

PART 2:
THREE BUILDING WORDS

→» «←

WORD #4:
TRUTH

-›- ‹-‹-

September 11, 2001, is a day in history that will never be forgotten—not by us, and not by the men who perpetrated the horrific bloodshed. Islamic terrorists hijacked four U.S. planes and wickedly crashed three of them into national landmarks. The fourth, bound for a target in Washington, D.C., crashed in rural Pennsylvania. Thousands of innocent Americans were murdered.

Difficult though it may be, try to picture for a moment in your mind's eye the final seconds before impact. What were those terrorists thinking? What was in their minds in the last few moments?

Well, if you think that their eyes were filled with fear, they were not. If you think that their stomachs were churning with anguish or that their mouths were drawn in horror, you'd be wrong. Anyone who understands their deviant brand of religion knows that they were probably grinning from ear-to-ear, because they believed they were dying in service to Allah. They were expecting to wake up in paradise, to receive a harem of beautiful young women, to experience eternal bliss, and to see the very face of God.

Instead, they woke up in hell, saw the face of Satan, and are now experiencing eternal torment. They pursued with earnest desire what they now know to be error and delusion. They were, of course, sincere in what they believed, but they were sincerely wrong! So the next time somebody says to you, "It doesn't matter what you believe as long as you are sincere," just say, "You're wrong! It matters incredibly what you believe!"

Many families with great sincerity are flying out-of-control and grinning ear-to-ear, yet in only a few weeks or months they will suddenly crash and perhaps never recover. They say, "We are sincere people. We love our kids and are doing the best we can." But sincerity alone can destroy you, too. The issue is not how much you care or how hard you work for your family. The question is, on what are you basing your judgments? What system of belief is informing the decisions you make and the actions you take? If you are not building your life on truth, then you are headed for a big-time crash no matter how sincere your intentions may be.

WHAT IS TRUTH?

Maybe you're cynically saying to yourself, like Pontius Pilate said in John 18:38, **"What is truth?"** In context, Jesus had been praying for His disciples, and by application for you and me. This is what He prayed in John 17:17, **"Sanctify them in the truth; Your word is truth."** Now I don't know about you, but I take very seriously the things that Jesus says. He prayed, **"Sanctify them."** The word *sanctify* means *change*. It is God's transforming process in the life of every believer. Jesus prayed, "Change them, Father; all My disciples, sanctify them." And then the second phrase, **"in the truth."** There's the fuel for change. What gas is to a motor, what gunpowder is to a fireworks display, what good food is to our bodies, truth is to transformation.

If you want to see change in your life and in your family, you must take hold of this matter of truth. But where is truth found? Jesus didn't leave any doubt about that: "**Your word is truth.**" This is what the Son prayed to the Father. Every word that proceeds from the mouth of God is absolute, authoritative, binding truth.

I could spend a lot of time going through the various ideas from science, medicine, sociology, psychology, and other disciplines that have been paraded in our world as truth, only later to be exposed as error. Here are just a few:

- *The center of the universe.* Aristotle (384–322 B.C.) believed that Earth was the center of the universe and that everything else revolved around it. This was the reigning scholarly view for nineteen centuries, until Copernicus demonstrated in 1530 that Earth and the other planets revolved around the Sun.[1]

- *Bloodletting.* For many centuries, bloodletting was considered a standard remedy for certain health conditions. It was recommended for fevers, inflammations, and (ironically) for hemorrhage. Although it fell in and out of favor, it persisted into the twentieth century and was even recommended by Sir William Osler in the 1923 edition of his *Principles and Practice of Medicine.*

- *Evolution.* Evolutionists have provided numerous examples of "truths" that were later exposed as errors. *Nebraska Man, Piltdown Man,* and *Java Man* were all put forward as missing links in the so-called evolutionary chain but were later discovered to be hoaxes. *Neanderthal Man* was reconstructed in 1915 by Marcellin Boule. Boule arranged the big toe to look like an opposing thumb and misplaced the knee joint, spine and head so the skeleton had a crouching, ape-like appearance. It was on display in Chicago's Field Museum of Natural History for forty-four years before someone detected what he had done. Even after the hoax was discovered, they kept it on display for another twenty years until they created a new Neanderthal model. Then, instead of discarding the skeleton, they moved it to a different floor under the title "An Alternate View of Neanderthal."[2]

BAG THE ERROR; EMBRACE THE TRUTH!

In place of this kind of shifting, sordid, pseudo-truth, I proclaim to you the living, abiding Word of God—always true, always reliable. As the Scriptures declare:

> **Teach me Your way, O Lord; I will walk in Your truth.** (Psalm 86:11)
>
> **All Your commandments are truth.** (Psalm 119:151)
>
> **The sum of Your word is truth, and every one of Your righteous ordinances is everlasting.** (Psalm 119:160)
>
> **In the exercise of His will He brought us forth by the word of truth.** (James 1:18)

Jesus Himself said, "**Heaven and earth will pass away, but My words will not pass away**" (Luke 21:33).

The Bible is the greatest book that has ever been written because it is the only book that God has written, preserved, protected, and promoted. It has the endorsements of the greatest minds throughout human history. God's Word has *never* been tried and found lacking. Never! However, it has often been found difficult and therefore not tried. There are people who throw out flippant comments such as, "Oh, the Bible is full of contradictions." OK, name one. "Well, uh, I'm not exactly sure—" That's always the statement of an ignorant person who has never studied the Word of God. Someone says, "I don't believe the Bible; it's out-of-date." Which part? Be specific!

No, the truths of the Bible have satisfied the greatest students in human history. The skeptic with little or no knowledge of Scripture is not even capable of framing a question about the Bible for which there is not a fairly simple and easily accessible answer. Don't ever let someone make you cower in your confidence regarding God's truth. For the most part, those who persistently question the Bible are not doing so because they object to its veracity, but rather because its message cuts to the very heart of their condition and points to a God who calls us all to account. The Bible is truth!

TRUTH IS WHERE THE ACTION IS.

Do you want a strong family? Do you want a family that is going to pass the test? Do you want a marriage that is going to make it to the finish line? Do you want kids who are going to rise up and call you blessed? That's what most of us desire, but so few people are getting it because their foundation is wrong. Maybe they invest a lot of time and energy in building their family, but if the foundation is wrong, it only takes a little storm before everything you've worked for comes crashing down upon your head.

Jesus tells a story to make this important point. Beginning in Matthew 7:24: "**Therefore everyone who hears these words of Mine and acts on them, may be compared to a wise man who built his house on the rock.**" Another word for *rock* there is *truth*. Then He continued:

> "**And the rain fell, and the floods came, and the winds blew and slammed against that house; and yet it did not fall, for it had been founded on the**

rock. Everyone who hears these words of Mine and does not act on them, will be like a foolish man who built his house on the sand. The rain fell, and the floods came, and the winds blew and slammed against that house; and it fell—and great was its fall." (verses 25–27)

Notice first, there are *two kinds of families.* There are families building on the rock, and those that are building on the sand; families building on the truth, and families building on the . . . ? Lies, neglect, apathy—I am not sure all that constitutes "sand," but it's not *truth.* Now on one level, there are some pretty attractive things about building your home on the sand. It's fast, it looks good on the outside, and your neighbors will be really impressed. "Sand castles" free up a lot of time for other stuff that brings more instant gratification. If you are building your family on the sand, you're like, "Get to work, boys, 'cause we're gonna have this whole thing up and be eating brats on the deck by 5:00 P.M.!" Building your family on the sand is fast and easy and appears for a time to be the way to go. That's why so many people get sucked into the sand scenario. In fact, I believe it's the default position. On the other hand, building your house on the rock—the truth—requires intentionality and focus. It seems like a big hassle: lots of time and effort to drill deep and build carefully upon the truth. And worst of all, until a major storm hits, it looks like the house built on truth was a lot of wasted effort.

Yes, two kinds of families, but notice secondly that there is only *one kind of experience.* **"And the rain fell, and the floods came, and the winds blew and slammed against that house."** Verse 25 looks a lot like verse 27. Two different families building their lives on two different foundations, but a very similar kind of experience. What family can you think of that has not encountered some storms? Your family is going to have some storms just as mine will. You say, "I think we're going to beat the odds." No, you're not! You will have many small storms, and no doubt several pretty large ones, hit your family during your lifetime. The storm might be a health crisis, or the tragic loss of someone close to you. It might be a major, sudden financial reversal, or it might be the rebellion of a son or daughter who breaks your heart. It's not hard to guess what it might be. What is hard is to believe that storms matter that much, because until they do come, all the houses and families on your street look pretty much the same. Only when the storms rage does it become apparent which families are built on the rock of truth, and which ones are built on the sand.

Third, there are *two kinds of outcomes*. The house on the sand had a great fall—total, sudden devastation. The house founded on the rock stood. Strong families are built on the truth. If that seems like a small thing to you, I assure you it is not. If you have never witnessed the total collapse of a family unit, I can tell you from experience that nothing is so painful or so permanent. As a pastor, I witness people going through just about every difficult circumstance that life can deal out, and by far the hardest "hand" to play is family collapse. When your marriage is over, when your kids are living in the world, when your finances are in ruin, when your spiritual life has crashed to the ground—well, it's just the worst kind of pain a person can experience. So here's some teaching from God's Word on how to avoid that pain by building your family on the truth.

BUILDING YOUR FAMILY ON TRUTH REQUIRES DILIGENCE.

If building your family on the truth were easy, everybody would be doing it—but many aren't. Diligence is absolutely necessary. In the book of 2 Timothy, the apostle Paul was writing to a young pastor named Timothy about building his ministry. By application, these truths also have much to say about building strong families. Look at what Paul wrote in 2 Timothy 2:14–15: **"Remind them of these things, and solemnly charge them in the presence of God not to wrangle about words, which is useless and leads to the ruin of the hearers. Be diligent to present yourself approved to God as a workman who does not need to be ashamed, accurately handling the word of truth."**

Yes, diligence is essential to building your family on the truth, but what kind of diligence?

DILIGENCE TO AVOID FOOLISH ISSUES

Notice that phrase in verse 14, **"Remind them of these things, and solemnly charge them."** In other words, this is serious business! God's got some stuff that He wants communicated. We need to be very focused on this. And charge them how?—**"in the presence of God."** The idea here is that we are not alone. Almighty God Himself is with us and is very intent on this message. He wants us all to hear it; so we'd better listen up.

"Charge them . . . not to wrangle about words." I wonder if there is anything that brings such devastation to our homes as wrangling about words. That word *wrangle* could be translated literally "a war of words." It's the silly, nonsensical, back-and-forth-and-back-and-forth arguing and blah, blah, blah of life. Anybody who provides marriage counseling knows that when a couple comes in and says, "Our thing is unraveling so bad that we have to come and talk to one of the pastors," nine times out of ten the pastor will listen for a short while and think to himself, *What's your deal? You're fighting about* what? *Your whole marriage is unraveling over this? You're kidding me, right?* Silly, secondary issues that are not substantive or significant, and that ought not to be tearing our homes apart.

Paul warns that wrangling about words **"is useless."** It's of no value; it's worthless. It's talk, talk, talk, talk, talk—wrangling about words. Let me ask you a question. Would you take your hard-earned money and invest it in a company if it were going bankrupt? It would be a waste of money, right? Would you bet on a racehorse (well, we don't bet on horses, but you know what I'm saying) with a broken leg? That would be a really bad decision. The concept in this verse is the very same. It's worthless to wrangle about words.

We only get so many words in our families. The older our kids get, the fewer words we have with them. What are you going to spend your words on? "Clean up your room!" "I asked you five times to take out the garbage!" "How many cookies have you had since lunch?" Is that how you're going to spend your words? Like that's going to have a big impact! I fear we're wasting our words on issues of little value, and then we're too exhausted to pour into our families the kind of truth that can be a fountain of life to them. Instead, let's choose words of truth that build and guide and that establish a foundation of wisdom for our families that will last them a lifetime.

Notice that when we fail to do so, it **"leads to the ruin of the hearers."** Can you imagine that? The word *ruin* comes from the Greek word *katastrophē*. It's not hard to figure out what English word comes from that. If you want to have a catastrophe on your hands, if you want to have kids in the world, finances in the toilet, and a marriage in the dumpster, wrangle about words. Quibble and argue about silly things.

God, give us the humility to go back to our children or spouse and say, "I am sorry. I have been pressing you about a matter that is not significant." We must have diligence to avoid foolish issues if we are going to build on the truth.

Diligence to Prioritize the Word of Truth

We also must be diligent to prioritize the Word of Truth. Look at verse 15: "**Be diligent to present yourself approved to God as a workman who does not need to be ashamed, accurately handling the word of truth.**" Notice that first phrase, "**Be diligent.**" The word literally means *make haste*. This is not a message to apply next year, or next month, or even next week. This is a message for today, for right now. Be diligent. Make haste.

And then, "**Present yourself approved to God**" regarding the Word of Truth. Do you realize that God knows how you are handling His Book? He knows. He knows whether you are attentive to it and leading your family by it, or whether you are digging it out and dusting it off for church on Sunday—or maybe not even that. God knows. The idea here is to be diligent to present yourself approved to God, because He is watching how you are handling the Word of Truth. It really matters!

Each of us needs to be "**a workman who does not need to be ashamed.**" If the truth were known, a lot of God's people are ashamed about their avoidance or ignorance of the Word of Truth. You say, "I hardly even know what the Bible says." Well, why don't you know? How long have you been a believer?

Have you had enough time to invest in the stock market? Have you had enough time to follow the World Series? You know a lot of other things! You follow some things in the newspaper very closely, but do you know the Word of Truth? There are things that are happening in your home and with your children that are not right. You haven't stood up and said, "This is the Word of Truth." We don't want to be ashamed by the way that we handle the Word of Truth, so we must be diligent.

I love this next part: "**accurately handling the word of truth.**" When I was a kid, I memorized this verse in the King James Version as "rightly dividing the word of truth." Actually, in the original Greek there's just one word. It's a compound word that means *cut it straight*. Don't you love that picture? We are supposed to be cutting it straight, rightly dividing, accurately handling the Word of Truth.

We need to cut it straight in our families. When my daughter wants to date an unbeliever—but the Word of Truth says in 2 Corinthians 6:14, "**Do not be bound together with unbelievers**"—I go to her and I cut it straight. When my son wants to listen to ungodly music in my house—but the Word of Truth says in Philippians 4:8, **"Whatever is pure, whatever is lovely . . . dwell on these things"**—I go to him and cut it straight.

Maybe you say, "Hey, to be honest with you, my marriage is not doing very well right now. It's more *work* than *wow*, for sure! I have to be honest and tell you that some days, in my darkest moments, I wonder if I can make it. I'm just not sure I can stick it out for the rest of my life." But the Word of Truth says in Matthew 19:6, **"What therefore God has joined together, let no man separate."** And so put that thinking out of your mind, and cut it straight.

Maybe you have been having a hard time at work, and the finances aren't what they used to be. This hasn't been a good year; sales are down, and you've been tempted to cut some corners. Maybe you've thought about withholding your giving to your church because you think, *God, I have to provide for my family and cover certain obligations.* You've been tempted to compromise the Word of Truth. But then you remember Matthew 6:33, **"But seek first His kingdom and His righteousness, and all these things will be added to you."** No longer will you allow yourself the luxury of wandering from what the Word of God says. You are "cutting it straight"; you are accurately handling the Word of Truth. And you are making the Word of God a priority.

Recently, we had some major rainstorms in our area. Many people had their basements completely flooded. The morning after the storm, two sweet sisters who live next door to us came by and said, "We were calling you on the phone in the middle of the night. We wanted to make sure your basement didn't flood."

"Well, we only have cordless phones," I said. "When the power went out, our phones didn't ring."

"Only a couple of cordless phones for a family your size?" the sisters answered. "We have six phones in our house: three cordless phones, and three regular phones."

I couldn't believe it. "Wow, you have *six* phones? For what?" They answered, "Well, we work for the phone company. What do you expect? Isn't your house full of Bibles?"

I laughed out loud, "Well, yes, as a matter of fact, it is!" I walked away smiling to myself because that's what I want our family to be known for—full of the truth of God's Word. That's what we are all about, building on God's Book, making it the priority. But that's not an easy thing to do.

BUILDING YOUR FAMILY
ON TRUTH REQUIRES CORRECTION.

You say, "But, James, if I take a stand like you just described, cutting it straight and all that in my marriage, there is going to be some conflict. If I start getting firmer with my kids about the truth, there is going to be some trouble!" That cannot be avoided, because building your family on truth requires correction.

Paul wrote about the Lord's servant—and certainly in our homes we are the Lord's servants—**"The Lord's bond-servant must not be quarrelsome, but be kind to all, able to teach, patient when wronged, with gentleness correcting those who are in opposition"** (2 Timothy 2:24–25).

Gentleness Amid Opposition

Those words "with gentleness" are so important. That is the manner in which we are to speak truth in our homes. When we pursue truth with gentleness, we safeguard our homes against harsh, brutal words that are really just thinly veiled personal hurt or frustration with a family member's problems. So correction comes with gentleness, but it does come. **"With gentleness correcting those who are in opposition."** A decision to diligently pursue truth in your home will bring opposition. Not maybe; for certain—and soon. You say, "What kind of opposition is coming my way?"

First, the *opposition of misunderstanding.* If you build your family on the truth, there is going to be some rejection. Maybe some of the members of your extended family are going to be like, "Man! You have just gone off the deep end with this Bible thing!" You may be accused of being harsh, no matter how loving you have been, simply because the Word of Truth cuts. You may have people judge your motives or attack your character, pointing out that, "Hey, you're not exactly perfect yourself."

There will be the *opposition of tiredness.* I remember Kathy and I went through this with our kids when they were a lot younger. "I am so tired from constantly teaching and training my kids in the truth," you say. "At times they seem to need an unending stream of correction, and it is exhausting!" Yes, I know how you feel, but don't let the opposition of tiredness stop you from doing what's right.

Then there's the *opposition of emotional distance.* Perhaps you have teenagers who call you uncool and unloving, and they won't see for many years the value of the truths on which you are building your family and refusing to compromise. I plead with you not to back down, no matter how many hurtful words they say or rolled eyes you must endure. In the major things, do what's right even if it sets off a war in your home. Draw the line. When your kids become adults and are raising their own kids, they will know that you did what was best for them. If you stick with it, someday they will thank you.

STANDING WHERE IT'S HARDEST

Now you might say, "I *am* standing for the truth at my house. I mean, I think I am. For the most part we are. At least in the *main* things we're standing for the truth. In the *big* stuff." No, *you are not standing for the truth unless you are doing so at the specific point where the truth is being resisted.* This is absolutely critical. Martin Luther, the father of the Protestant Reformation, once wrote: "If I profess with loudest voice and clearest exposition every portion of God's Word, except precisely that little point the world and the devil are that moment attacking, I am not professing Christ. Where the battle rages, there the loyalty of the soldier is proved. And to be steady on all the battlefront beside but compromise there is merely flight and disgrace."[3] Luther is right, and the Christian families of our day desperately need to heed his challenge.

You can be standing for the truth in fifteen different places, but if you are conceding at the very point of opposition, you are not building your home on the truth. It only takes one leak to create a flood of compromise. What is that point of opposition in your home or in your marriage or with your kids right now? Where is the battle raging? Stand firm at that place. You say, "There's going to be conflict." Then have it! That is the exact place where the Word of Truth needs to come to bear upon your home.

But why? Why do we stand on the truth? Why go through such potential hardship? Because it is only when we stand on the truth that we work in partnership with God. Notice what it says in verse 25: **"With gentleness correcting those who are in opposition, if perhaps God may grant them repentance leading to the knowledge of the truth."** You say, "I want my marriage to be changed. I want my kids to be changed. I want my parents to be changed. I want to reach my brother for Christ." When you wield the truth, then you are in partnership with God. When you get truth on the table, then

God may grant them repentance. That's the first step in all change—genuine repentance—and only God can produce it.

Unless you are brokering truth, God is not supporting the investments you are making in your family relationships. If this is sounding intense and harsh, keep reading.

BUILDING YOUR FAMILY ON TRUTH REQUIRES RELATIONSHIP.

You say, "But I love my family. Truth seems so cold and so separated from relationship." No, that can never be. On the contrary, I would suggest that building your family on truth demands loving, meaningful relationships. That's so important.

RELATIONSHIP WITH THE LEARNER

Paul discussed the connection between truth and family relationships in 2 Timothy 3:14–16. First, there must be a relationship with the learner. Here's verse 14: **"You, however, continue in the things you have learned and become convinced of, knowing from whom you have learned them."** Take a moment and read that verse again. Do you see anything strange? There is something in there that I would not have expected to see. I would have expected Paul to say, "Timothy, keep on going in the things you have learned, knowing *what* you have learned." But that is not what he says. I would have anticipated Paul to say, "Timothy, keep on going in the things you have learned, knowing *how* you learned them. You *do* remember all the stuff you had to go through to learn this, don't you? Do you want to go through that again?" But again, that is not what Paul says. My third choice would have been, "Timothy, keep on going in the things you have learned, knowing *why* you learned them. Everyone knows the importance of remembering the lessons we learn during hardship." But he doesn't say that either.

The thing Paul highlights is this: "Timothy, keep on going in the things you have learned, knowing *from whom* you learned them." Paul says, "Hey, do you know what's really important? It's the relationship." What matters most is not what or how or why Timothy learned—it's *who* did the teaching that was paramount.

You say to yourself, "Well, of course he would say that. I mean, if the apostle Paul had been my teacher, I think *who* taught me would have been really important, too. But I didn't have a teacher like that." Hold on! Paul wasn't talking about himself teaching Timothy, because in the beginning of the next verse, he references Timothy's childhood: **"Knowing from whom you have learned them, and that from childhood you have known the sacred writings."**

Who teaches the members of our family truth is a very important matter, and it must not be overlooked. And who had taught Timothy? Flip back to 2 Timothy 1:5, where Paul wrote, **"For I am mindful of the sincere faith within you, which first dwelt in your grandmother Lois and your mother Eunice, and I am sure that it is in you as well."** That ought to encourage every single parent. Timothy's father was Greek and apparently did not worship the God of Israel (Acts 16:1, 3), but Timothy had a faithful mother and grandmother who poured truth into his life. It is absolutely vital for us to understand that truth is most powerfully taught in the context of relationship.

I remember a family from the church where I grew up. The mother was very musical and played an instrument in every worship service. The father was there with his kids every time the doors of the church opened. He even taught the truth at home over the dinner table and lived a life of integrity. But he was not a friend to his kids. He was cold and harsh and distant. He was often angry, and he consistently and increasingly withheld himself from his kids as they began to rebel against his "rules without relationship." Suffice it to say, some of his kids did not come back to the Lord until they were in their mid-thirties, and others have still not come back.

The father may be with the Lord by now, but sadly some of his kids may never be because truth was not taught in the context of relationship.

It is not your pastor's job to teach the Word of God to your kids. It is not the AWANA leader's job. It is not the Sunday School teacher's or the youth worker's responsibility. Praise God for those supplemental things. But it is our job as parents to teach our children the Word of God.

Parents, if you are getting that done, I just want to encourage you. Even if your kids struggle, even if they wander, I believe with all of my heart that they are coming back. They won't stay away forever. The blessing will bring them back, and they will return to the truths that you have over many years poured into their hearts—provided you taught that truth in the context of a relationship.

I am still learning this lesson myself. Just recently, I was starting a new Bible study with my oldest son. I said to Luke, "Why don't we study the life of David. Here's the book." After doing the first chapter, he came back to me and said, "Dad, I don't really want to do this study right now." He had never said anything like that to me before. "Couldn't we just go for a drive, and then we could talk, and then maybe we could pray together at the end?" I was reminded of the very thing we're learning here, "It's about the relationship." Truth is taught in the context of a relationship.

Relationship with the Author

Not only is it important to have a relationship with the learner, but also with the Author. Take note of what Paul says at the end of 2 Timothy 3:14–15: **"Continue in the things you have learned and become convinced of, knowing from whom you have learned them, and that from childhood you have known the sacred writings which are able to give you the wisdom that leads to salvation through faith which is in Christ Jesus."** At the end of the day, it's all about Jesus Christ. We do not worship the Bible. At one level, we are not even particularly interested in the Bible, except that the Bible conveys the truth about Christ. Do you get that? It is not the Book; it is the Person in the Book.

From the Bible we learn about the Savior. Jesus said to the Pharisees in John 5:39, **"You search the Scriptures because you think that in them you have eternal life; it is these that testify about Me."** It is about the Author.

We used to sing a chorus when we were little kids:

The Bible is the written Word of God.
It tells about the living Word of God.
On every page, on every line,
You will find the Son of God divine.

It's all about Jesus Christ. It is essential that we remember this. All worship flows from knowing the Christ of Scripture. All comfort flows from knowing the Christ of God's Word. All grace and goodness and blessing and joy flow from knowing the Person who is revealed in the Book.

FAMILIES BUILT ON TRUTH PREVAIL.

Do you want to win the most important battle in life—the battle for your family? Do you want to get through the tough things you are facing right now? Get your family anchored on the truth. One of my favorite passages is 2 Timothy 3:16–17: "**All Scripture is inspired by God and profitable for teaching, for reproof, for correction, for training in righteousness.**" *Inspired* comes from the Greek word that means *God-breathed*. In other words, God didn't just choose some concepts and tell the authors of Scripture, "Hey, write some stuff about this." No, God chose the very words of Scripture. "**Men moved by the Holy Spirit spoke from God**" (2 Peter 1:21)—word for word from the heart of God. That's why I prefer to study a precise translation of the Bible.

All Scripture—from Genesis 1:1 to Revelation 22:21—is inspired by God and profitable for four things: *teaching* (doctrinal truth about God and salvation and money and work and family); *reproof* (the Bible points out our faults and shows us the error of our ways); *correction* (the Bible also shows us the right things—it's not just "Don't do this" but also "Do this"); and *training in righteousness* (not just what to do but how to do it; the right course of action and how to get there).

Building Strong Families Ten Ways

All in favor of building our families on the truth? Let me give you ten practical ideas with the hope that you will actually choose to do two or three of them. Fire these up in your home. Do them today. If you are a single adult, then fire these up with your roommate. Wherever your family is right now, get this going.

1. *Start a regular time of family Bible reading and prayer.* Just say, "Hey, from now on, Monday nights at our house, we get the Book open. Right after dinner, we spend some time reading and praying together."
2. *Memorize a portion of God's Word as a family.* Just say, "Hey, we are a newly married couple, and we are going to build our home on the truth." Psalm 127 or Ephesians 6 would be good places to start.

3. *Have a contest to learn the books of the Bible.* After all, it's hard to find the location without knowing the addresses! "We are all going to learn the books of the Bible together, and then there are going to be prizes at the end." Make them good prizes, Dad, don't be cheap! Learn the books of the Bible together.

4. *Read through the Bible in a year.* You say, "My kids are getting a little older now," or, "We are a young couple," or, "Me and my roommate are going to read through the Bible together in a year. We are going to talk about it as we go and help each other."

5. *Get a series of cassette tapes on the family.* You say, "I think we need a little tune-up." OK, get a teaching series. Most pastors and Bible teachers have taught on marriage and the family. Purchase the message, sit down at a regular time, open your Bibles, listen to the tape, make some notes, and pray about it and discuss it afterwards.

6. *Make decisions about family matters from the Bible.* If you're facing a big decision, go and ask your pastor, "Where is a passage we could read that would really help us make this decision?"

7. *Turn off the television and read a Bible story out loud with enthusiasm!* "Hey, kids, come here. You think that show's good? Listen to this!" Find a story in the Old Testament: "You cannot believe what God was doing here!" Let them see that Mom and Dad are fired up about the truth that is in the Book.

8. *Attend a Bible study or class together.* Attend as a couple. Attend as a family. Learn from God's Word.

9. *Don't just pray with your kids before bed, but read a portion of God's Word to them.* Open the Bible, show them what the Word of God says, *then* pray with them and tuck them into bed. Deuteronomy 6:7 says, "**You shall teach [God's commands] diligently to your sons and shall talk of them when you sit in your house and when you walk by the way and when you lie down and when you rise up.**"

10. *Choose some family values and post them at home.* The MacDonald family has five family values, and we just finished having them painted in a beautiful mural on our family room wall where they are always before our eyes. Here they are (feel free to use them or create your own):

I. *Love God.* Big surprise! How straight up is that, right? What is the greatest commandment in Scripture? **"Love the Lord your God with all your heart"** (Mark 12:30).

II. *Family first.* "Don't talk to your sister like that." "That's your mother; do what she says!" "We are together in this, and we'll get through together." Loyalty, commitment, unity, vision, family first.

III. *Work hard.* My middle name is Sherwood, my mother's maiden name. As a kid, my mom would pull me really close and whisper in my ear, "Sherwoods know how to work. Don't you ever forget that. We know how to work hard." I would be doing a little job around the house and she would speak my middle name, a symbol of a character trait given to her that she in turn was modeling and demanding of me. What a great vision to give our children in this lazy, selfish world—work hard!

IV. *Tell the truth.* Even when it's painful. Even when it's going to get you into more trouble. Just get the truth on the table. God can do a lot with that. Don't mess with truth, don't measure truth, don't muddle truth. Just model it and mouth it. Truth will get you to all the right places as a family. God Himself will make sure of that. And finally,

V. *Be kind.* "We are not going to talk about them like that. That's not kind." Don't run people down, don't run people over, don't run people around. Just be kind and treat others the way you want to be treated. Just being kind by itself will solve a lot of problems.

These are our family values; use them or get your own. Just be sure to have some and post them in your house.

READY FOR THE VOYAGE

Why should you do all of this? Second Timothy 3:17: **"So that the man of God may be adequate, equipped for every good work."** That text of Scripture actually means *thoroughly equipped for the voyage of life.* God's Word contains all the truth we need to be thoroughly equipped for the voyage of life. Think of it: my spouse *thoroughly equipped for the voyage of life.* My son *thoroughly equipped for the voyage of life.* My daughter *thoroughly equipped for the voyage of life.* Our entire family *thoroughly equipped for the voyage of life.*

All that flows from your commitment to building your family on the truth.

A PRAYER TO GO HIGHER

Lord, thank You for showing me very clearly what it means to build my family and my marriage and my very life upon the truth of Your Word. In the areas where I'm not living up to Your standards, convict me, O God. May I not simply feel the importance of truth, but may I act upon it. Help me to be different today. Give me strength to persevere in the truth, even when doing so brings difficulties into my life. May I show respect for Your truth by determining to act upon what I've learned. These things I pray in the strong name of Your Son, Jesus Christ. Amen.

A PROJECT TO GO DEEPER

Psalm 119 proclaims the splendor of God's Word and the blessings that come from living according to its truth. Over the next few days, read and meditate your way through this lengthy psalm (176 verses). Jot down your observations. What is life like for those who follow God's commands? How is it different for those who choose to do their own thing? Of what value is God's Word?

Be sure to journal the things that the Lord is teaching you.

A PRACTICE TO GO FURTHER

I concluded this chapter by suggesting ten simple and practical things that you could do to help build your family on the truth. Well, what are you waiting for? Within the next week, choose at least three of these ideas and start putting them into practice. And don't be concerned if things don't go as smoothly as you would like the first time. Just do what you know is right, and trust God to bring about the change that He wants in your family. Once you've implemented three suggestions, you'll be ready to go to the next chapter.

NOTES

1. Even though Copernicus had a better handle on the truth, he still believed that the sun was the center of the universe, which was later disproved.
2. Erik Trinkhaus, "Pathology and the Posture of the La Chappelle-aux-Saints Neanderthal." *American Journal of Physical Anthropology* 67 (1985): 19–41. This article was cited at the Smithsonian Institute's website, www.mnh.si.edu/anthro/humanorigins/aop/aop_start.html.
3. As cited in Francis A. Schaffer, *Complete Works*, vol. 2 (Wheaton, Ill.: Crossway, 1982), 122.

WORD #5:
CHURCH

⤛ ⤜

The church of Jesus Christ is, without a doubt, the most neglected family resource in the world today. All around us are families trying with all their might to become all that they can be in the Lord. Yet many are doing so without the help of the only institution God created to nurture and support the family.

Consider, for example, the material we covered in the last chapter on truth. What are the chances of building your family on the truth without meaningful connectedness to a Bible-believing, local church? Answer: zero! It is impossible! Your family will never make it on its own. A family left to itself cannot possibly live out what God's Word teaches with any kind of consistency. That is why God has placed us in communities of faith called local churches.

Look at what Paul wrote in 1 Timothy 3:15 concerning the church: "**I write so that you will know how one ought to conduct himself in the household of God, which is the church of the living God, the pillar and support of the truth.**" Notice that the church is the pillar of the truth. What does a *pillar* do? It holds up the roof. Many families today feel like the roof is falling in on top of them, but it doesn't need to be that way. Notice also that the church is the *foundation* of the truth. It's a strong support that will allow the truth to stand in your home during times of hardship that shake your family to its very core.

Clearly, as both the pillar and foundation of God's truth, the church must not be neglected in our families if we want to experience His transforming power. The church of Jesus Christ is an incredible resource to help your marriage, train your children, and enlarge your family's capacity to receive all the blessings God wants to give. And yet the average family is missing out on the tremendous wealth and protection and covering that are available in the local church. No doubt about it; the most overlooked resource is the church.

But don't miss why Paul penned these words: **"so that you will know how one ought to conduct himself in the household of God."** The sad fact is that most family members don't have a clue how to mine for themselves the benefits that are available in a meaningful connection to the local church. And because they don't know how to "conduct themselves," they are missing out on immense blessing from the Lord. That's the problem we are going after in this chapter.

I want to share three simple things to help you access the benefits of this fifth word to change your family: (1) Believe in the church, (2) submit to the church, and (3) participate in the church.

You say, "I have to be honest, James. I don't think our family is getting much out of our church the way we should. How can we improve in that?" Well, it starts here.

BELIEVE IN THE CHURCH.

That's the first thing. You have to believe in the church, like Jesus does. Look at Matthew 16:13–15:

> **Now when Jesus came into the district of Caesarea Philippi, He was asking His disciples, "Who do people say that the Son of Man is?" And they said, "Some say John the Baptist; and others, Elijah; but still others, Jeremiah, or one of the prophets." He said to them, "But who do you say that I am?"**

That's always the big question—who do *you* say that Jesus is? It doesn't matter who your mom thinks Jesus is, or who your grandpa thinks Jesus is, or who your neighbor thinks Jesus is. The question is, "Who do *you* think Jesus is?" That's what it's all about.

So Jesus turned to the disciples and said, **"Who do you say that I am?"** The text says, **"Simon Peter answered"** (verse 16). Now that's not a surprise because Peter was always pretty quick with something to say. He would jump in at random times and say all kinds of wild, off-the-wall things that left everyone else scratching their heads. But you know how it is in baseball—if you keep coming to the plate over and over, eventually you're going to make contact with the ball. And this time he nailed it: **"Simon Peter answered, 'You are the Christ, the Son of the living God.'"** Peter hit a home run—a grand slam! **"And Jesus said to him, 'Blessed are you, Simon . . . because flesh and blood did not reveal this to you, but My Father who is in heaven'"** (verse 17).

GOD IN PURSUIT

Let me ask you a question. How does a person come to know Christ personally? A lot of people think that it happens through various levels of human persuasion. "Well, if you could just be clever in how you present the gospel, you are going to reach a lot of people." Wrong! If you have turned from your sin and embraced Christ by faith as the only basis for your forgiveness, the only reason why you even have a clue is because God pursued you. God was like, "We'll take her." He opened your eyes, and all of a sudden you got it!

Why hasn't your coworker or your next door neighbor gotten it? Because God hasn't opened his or her eyes yet. The Bible tells us, **"The god of this world has blinded the minds of the unbelieving so that they might not see the light of the gospel of the glory of Christ"** (2 Corinthians 4:4). Jesus made it clear why Peter got it: **"Flesh and blood did not reveal this to you, but My Father who is in heaven."**

A SOLID ROCK

Then Jesus made this key statement about the church: **"I also say to you that you are Peter, and upon this rock I will build My church"** (Matthew 16:18).

That is quite a statement from the Lord Jesus Christ, but it has caused a lot of confusion down through the ages. For fifteen hundred years, this verse has been used by the Roman Catholic Church to teach that Peter was the first pope and the bishop of Rome. I pastor a nondenominational church, and I don't want to bash this group or that one. But I think it is important to understand that this passage is *not* teaching that Peter was the first pope, or that there is some succession of church leadership that came through Peter, or that when the pope speaks *ex cathedra,* just write it down because it's equal with Scripture. That is not what this passage teaches.

Here are three reasons for you to reject the "Peter was the first pope" thing. First, notice the phrase, "You are Peter, and upon this rock." That is actually a play on words in the original Greek. The word *Peter* in Greek is *petros,* which can mean *a very small stone.* The word *rock* in the original is *petra,* which means a great outcropping of rock. Notice the similarity? So, in effect, Jesus said, "Peter, you are a little stone, but upon this massive rock I will build my church!" Second, the earliest church fathers, including Origen, did not believe this passage was teaching that the church would be built on Peter himself, but rather on Peter's *confession.* In other words, the church of Jesus Christ would be built upon the truth that Peter had proclaimed. Third, even though Peter is recognized in the book of Acts as a leader in the early church, he certainly was not the singular leader, but just one of the apostles. Further, Ephesians 2:20 teaches that the apostles were foundational and unique for the church, so there aren't apostles in every generation, and there aren't bishops or popes that follow one after the other. The Bible does not teach that—not in any way.

The bottom line is, Jesus said, "Hey, Peter, you are a little man who said a big thing! I am going to build My church on what you said." And isn't that exactly what has happened? The church of Jesus Christ has been built upon the fact that Jesus is not just a man, not simply a good moral teacher, but that He is the Christ, the Son of the living God.

HE'S BUILDING HIS CHURCH.

With that said, let me point out that the controversy around this passage has caused many people to miss two incredible statements about the church. Here is the first one: **"I will build My church."** Just think about that. Jesus Christ said that He *will* build His church. Isn't that fantastic news? I don't know what you've been doing this week, but Jesus Christ has been building His church.

The word *church* comes from a compound word that means *the called-out ones.* "Called out of what?" you ask. Called out of the world. God was like, "Hey, you! Come on out of the world! Leave your sin behind. It's taking you nowhere. Come on over here! Be with Me. I am building a kingdom. You can be part of it." If you haven't heard that call, you can hear it today. Be reconciled to God through repentance and faith.

Perhaps you say, "We don't really believe in the church. My wife and I, we are really into *Jesus*, but we don't need the church thing. You know, bananas for Jesus, but we'll take a pass on the church!" Have you ever heard that? Every time I do I want to say, "Well, if you are really so 'into Jesus,' you oughta be into His church, too, because He sure is." In fact, Ephesians 5:25 says, **"Christ also loved the church and gave Himself up for her."** Christ *loves* the church. If you love Christ, you have to love His church, because that is what He is all about in this world.

You say, "We had a bad experience. We used to go to church, but we quit. We used to be involved, but now we are sort of sitting on the sidelines." Let me ask you a question. Have you ever had a bad meal at a restaurant? I mean like, "I cannot believe we paid for that! That was awful! That was dog food!" Or have you ever gone to a store and been sold something, and later you were like, "Man, I got *so* ripped off!" Has that ever happened to you? Of course it has, but you still eat at restaurants, don't you? "Just not at that restaurant anymore!" Do you still buy things from stores? "Yes, but I would never buy anything from *that* person again!" In the same way, I still believe in the church of Jesus Christ. I am not going to be turned off just because I've been hurt or wounded. I am not going to throw out the baby with the bathwater.

Jesus is for the church. Yes, it has sinful people in it, and it doesn't always work perfectly, but I believe in the church because Jesus promised, "I will build My church."

WE'RE GONNA WIN!

Then notice this second important statement in Matthew 16:18: **"The gates of Hades will not overpower it."** I *love* that! We're gonna win! When I was a kid, I used to play football with my friends at lunch hour—spring, winter, fall, every day. By the time I was in the third grade, I realized that it was way more fun to be on the winning team than on the losing team. So, with my little leadership gift (ha, ha!), I made up some teams and a schedule, ran off some copies, and got the boys organized. Nobody had a better plan, so everybody went along with the teams that I made up. Now how good do you suppose my team was? You better believe I was on a winning team! How else would you set things up if you were in charge?

I think there is a desire within each of us to be part of something that we know is headed in the right direction—something that's going to win. That's the church of Jesus Christ. The Lord said, "The gates of hell will not prevail against My church." When you stand in heaven someday, you want to be able to say, "I was on the winning team! I poured all of my effort and all of my energy into the things that Jesus said would succeed." If you want your family to win, too, get them in the middle of the church of Jesus Christ, because it is going to prevail. Jesus promised it would.

That's why I believe in the church. I don't believe in liberal churches. I don't believe in apostate churches. I don't believe in cults. I don't even believe in denominations. I know there are some helpful things there, but I don't put my faith in them. But with my whole heart, I believe in the church of Jesus Christ. I believe in the blood-bought, born-again, Spirit-filled army of the redeemed, and I am so thankful that my family is growing together under that protective umbrella. Is yours?

The church of Jesus Christ is an incredible resource for your family—full of truth and relationships and fellowship and support and accountability. If you would march your family to the very center of this thing called the church, the odds of having a successful, God-honoring family would be much more in your favor.

It has to start with you believing in the church. Do you? If so, you'll need this next thing to get all the good the church has to offer your family.

SUBMIT TO THE CHURCH.

There's the second part of accessing the benefits of the church for your family. You need to submit to the church. Now I can guess what you're thinking: *James, you are going way too far. I was tracking with you big-time until you had to get that ugly word out there*—submit. *I can hardly get that done at* home, *and now you want me to get that done at* church!? But what does Scripture say? **"Obey your leaders and submit to them, for they keep watch over your souls as those who will give an account. Let them do this with joy and not with grief, for this would be unprofitable for you"** (Hebrews 13:17).

Our culture equates authority with evil, abuse, and heavy-handed arrogance, but the leaders in God's church are not to be that way. First Peter 5 and Titus 1 teach that church leaders—the biblical terms are *elder* or *pastor*—are to be loving shepherds, examples to the flock, and servants. They should be sensible, devout, and self-controlled. The Bible teaches that you and your family are to find leaders like that in a church and place yourselves under their care.

Unless It's Sin, Obey Them

You say, "But I can't submit to the leaders if I don't agree with them." Yes, you can. Unless they are asking you to sin or do something that would dishonor the Lord, you ought to do the things that they are asking you to do. And if a leader of your church actually asks you to sin? Find a new church. The apostles were really clear about that: **"We must obey God rather than men"** (Acts 5:29). But unless it goes that far, you ought to fall in line. God will honor that, even if you don't see how at the moment.

Let me make something clear. When Scripture calls you to obey your leaders and submit to them, it is *not* talking about being a doormat. It's talking about obeying the things they teach you and the methods of ministry they call the church to implement. Consider for a moment just how many hours you have spent sitting under the teaching of God's Word in your own church, or how many hours you have spent reading Christian books like this one that explain portions of God's Word and call you to align your life with it. Now here's the big question: What have you done with what you've heard? As the truth is taught, you can't just sit there and say, "Oh, that's nice. There's something else I understand." No, you must obey it; you must *do* the things you are taught—not based on human authority, but based on the authority that God has given to the leaders in the church. Check the Scripture yourself, and if it's in God's Word, get it done.

Make It Easy for Them

Obey your leaders and submit to them. Why? **"For they keep watch over your souls"** (Hebrews 13:17). How great it is to have someone keeping watch over *your* soul! Think for a moment about the burden you feel just for your own family. Now imagine that instead of being burdened like you are for the per-haps *five* people in your family, you had to be burdened for *fifty* people! Or imagine that instead of carrying the responsibility for fifty people, you had to carry the responsibility for *five hundred* people! Or, in the case of the church that I pastor, imagine that you had the responsibility to watch over the souls of *five thousand* people! I can tell you that the burden is immense. This is why we are exhorted in God's Word to make it easy for those who are called to watch over us spiritually.

Church leaders who take their roles seriously are carrying a huge load, and you are in a position to help them help you by doing the things they teach you to do with a willing, submissive heart.

The reason church leaders are to fulfill their roles with diligence is because they "will give an account." For me, that's where the heaviness comes—from the realization that someday I am going to stand before God to account not only for my own life, but also for the lives of every person who has been under the care of our church. God is going to ask me and our other leaders about every sheep in our flock: "Did you teach them the truth? Did you challenge them to do what was right? Did you let them off easy and just give them a Sunday morning grin session? Or did you challenge them to live according to God's Word and to build their families on the Rock?"

Looking for FAT Christians

That's pretty heavy for church leaders, and here's the heavy part for you and your family.

"Let them [lead you] with joy and not with grief, for this would be unprofitable for you." The idea is pretty straightforward: Allow your church leaders to watch over you with joy. What makes a person a joy to lead? At our church, we call them FAT Christians (no offense!). They are *Faithful, Available,* and *Teachable.* Those people are a joy to lead. Faithful: every week in the same place. Available: "Call me anytime. I'll cancel my plans if I need to because my number one priority is to serve God." And teachable: "Was I wrong? Thanks for pointing that out; I'll work on that." Teachable people are humble enough that every corrective moment does not become a wrestling match. FAT Christians bring joy to every pastor's heart.

On the other hand, there are a few people who, far from being a joy to lead, are a source of grief. Critical, negative, faultfinding, complaining, unmoldable, unteachable attitudes—all the opposites of what we just discussed. Now, who loses if you behave like that? What does Hebrews 13:17 say? Does the church leader lose? No, you lose! The last line of the verse says, **"For this would be unprofitable for you."**

Think about it for a moment. Who gets the lion's share of the attention? The FAT Christians or the grief-causing Christians? Eventually, the church leaders begin to say (like Jesus did), "I think I am going to pour my energy into the faithful, available, teachable people. After all, I only have so many hours in the week, and I want to maximize my return." Church members who are a joy to lead will reap far more of the benefits Christ wants to give them through their church.

THE CHURCH—A GREAT BACKUP PLAN

You say, "What does this have to do with my family?" Here it is: When the authority structure in the home fails, the church is there to back it up. My wife, Kathy, and I built a new house a couple of years ago. Since then, I've had this sick feeling in the back of my mind: "I need to get a backup pump for my sump pump." And every time there would be a heavy rain, I'd be kicking myself for not buying one. But we'd make it through without any problems, and I would pledge to go out and get that backup pump. Well, I finally got one—just in time for some torrential rainstorms. I went down into my basement, and yes, my backup pump was working! It was such a feeling of relief. The main pump stopped when the power went out, but the backup pump with the special battery power kicked in. I avoided a flooded basement like so many of my neighbors.

Sometimes we need that in our home. Sometimes the authority structure in the home fails. What is your backup plan?

If you're plugged into the life of the church, when the authority structure in your home fails, the authority structure in the church will be there to back it up. And make no mistake, the authority structure in the home does fail. Everything is going along great, when all of a sudden Dad starts thinking he would be happier if he were living with some other woman. What are you going to do now? Dad bails out of the home, and there is a huge blowup. If you're not plugged into the church, what are you going to do if a son or daughter goes off the deep end? What's your support system if you have a serious financial crisis or a conflict at home that just cannot be resolved? As I think back over our church's thirteen-year history, I can picture countless families where, when the people were plugged into the church and the authority structure in their home failed, the church was able to step in and get things back on track.

I will never forget when a family in our church came to me several years ago. They were really struggling with their ten- or eleven-year-old son. He was rebellious and wouldn't do *anything* they told him to do. They said, "We can't deal with him! Can you help us with him?" I said, "Bring him into my office, and I'll talk to him." And they brought him in. This little boy comes walking into my office. I said very sternly, "Sit down over there! What is going on in your house?"

"Well, I just, I just, I don't—"

"Let me just tell you something." I went off and set him straight with a level of intensity perhaps he had never felt before. I put the fear of God into that boy! **"The fear of the Lord is the beginning of wisdom"** (Psalm 111:10). But before he left, I called him over and pulled him up on my lap. I looked into his eyes, and I told him how much we loved him and why he had to change. As I prayed, I began to weep over him and call upon the Lord to change his heart; and God has answered those prayers. Praise God, that encounter took place many years ago, and now that young man is walking with the Lord. The whole direction of his life was altered because, when the authority structure in his home failed, the authority structure of his church was there to back it up.

FEELING HASSLED AT TIMES?

Now, it can be a hassle at times having people involved in your life like that. I remember when Luke was maybe three or four years old. He had fallen and scraped his face, and after a couple of days, he had quite the black eye. There were these two ladies in our church who were part of the "grief brigade"—sort of cranky all the time, if you know what I mean. They were always jumping to strange conclusions about all kinds of things, and I was afraid they would think something weird about Luke's eye. So I pulled him aside before we went to church and said, "Luke, when we get to church, if these ladies come up and start drilling you, just tell them you fell down the stairs while you were playing. Just tell them what happened, and don't be nervous."

We rehearsed the details until I was confident that he could be clear. I said, "Now just be open and honest. Don't freak out or act weird or anything like that." So Luke was like, "OK, Dad. I got it."

Sure enough, we came out of church, and there were these two ladies. They walked up and said, "Luke! Luke! What happened to your eye?" And he froze! He just stopped dead in his tracks and didn't say a word, so I squeezed his hand for some reassurance. Then he looked up at me and said, "What did you tell me to say again, Dad?" Can you believe that? It was one of those awful moments. Anyway, long ago the Lord moved those two ladies on to give another pastor grief.

Maybe you have had a few negative experiences at church, and you think your family would be better off without the accountability, without all those people taking an interest in what your family is all about. If you think that, you are wrong. In spite of the occasional hassle my family gets at church, we are far better off than we would ever be without all the good we receive from the church. And if we would ever get into a really tough spot as a family, I am thankful that our church would be there to back us up and make sure that God's priorities are being advanced in our home.

All of that to say this: Sometimes the church doesn't work perfectly. But ninety-five times out of a hundred, it is an incredible blessing and a wonderful resource. It brings great joy; it provides much needed accountability; and it gives you connectedness. I exhort you to get your family into the center of the church. Believe in the church. Submit to the church. And . . .

PARTICIPATE IN THE CHURCH.

This is the third, and perhaps most important, way to access the benefits of the church. In Hebrews 10, after celebrating the riches of Christ, the author writes, **"Therefore, brethren, since we have confidence to enter the holy place by the blood of Jesus."** The *holy place* is the place where God resides. We can come to Him because of the atoning work of Christ on the cross.

The author goes on to say, **"We have confidence to enter the holy place by the blood of Jesus, by a new and living way which He inaugurated for us through the veil, that is, His flesh"** (verses 19–20). In Old Testament times, a veil separated people from the presence of God. When Christ died, the veil in the temple was torn in two. But now there is a new veil; it's Christ Himself.

He is the way in, but He is also the One who keeps out of heaven people who won't enter by Him. Verse 21: **"And since we have a great priest over the house of God"**—because we have this phenomenal thing in Christ—we are to do three things.

Draw Near

First, we are to draw near: **"Let us draw near with a sincere heart in full assurance of faith, having our hearts sprinkled clean from an evil conscience and our bodies washed with pure water"** (verse 22). That's a statement about worship—drawing near to God. In other words, there is absolutely no barrier now between you and God. You have been washed clean. Isn't that a great thing? You say, "But I don't feel clean." That's why the author phrased it, **"in full assurance of faith."** It doesn't matter how you feel; you *are* clean! God loves you and has set His grace upon you. There is nothing that should hinder your worship of Him. It doesn't matter where you sit, but you ought to be moving forward in your worship. You ought to be growing in your capacity to express worship to God.

All biblical churches have as their centerpiece a weekend worship service where the believers come together to connect with God. A weekly, corporate God encounter can do more to turn up the spiritual temperature in your family than anything else. Here are some things you can do to maximize your family's weekly worship:

1. *Come together.* Someone has said, "Families that pray together stay together." I agree, and prayer is only one of the forms of worship that you should find in a good church. Get ready for church together, arrive together, sit together, leave together, and discuss together what the Lord was doing in all of your hearts afterwards.

2. *Come often.* How often do you attend your church? "Two out of three, maybe three out of four." No! Come every week. "But my mother-in-law is in town." Bring her to church! "She doesn't want to go." Then leave her at home, and you come! Come often.

3. *Come early.* In our church, it always seems like a herd of buffaloes come running two minutes before the start of each service. And then there's a big bottleneck, with people running and making each other crazy. "I

only yelled at three people in the parking lot today. I am ready to worship!" No, you're not! Come early.

4. *Come prepared.* Can I challenge you, Mom or Dad, to pray with your family before you come to church? Read a portion of Scripture. Stop in the driveway and say, "We're heading off to worship God; let's get our hearts ready." Start at Psalm 100, and read a psalm each week. Pray that the time of worship will be meaningful for your family.

I'll never understand why parents are so slow to figure out that their children are watching them worship. If your kids are in junior high or above, I could pull them aside and get a very detailed opinion from them about the sincerity of your love for God. A big part of their perspective is based on watching you worship. Your kids are right beside you. This is a commercial for God! Are you fired up about God and enthused about the truth that is found in Him and worshiping in spirit and in truth, or are you distant and apathetic and critical? In either case, your nonverbals are sending a huge message to your kids. You want to participate in the life of the church? You want to bring your family to the center of the church? Worship Christ. Draw near with full assurance of faith.

HOLD FAST WITHOUT WAVERING

Second, we are to hold fast without wavering: **"Let us hold fast the confession of our hope without wavering, for He who promised is faithful"** (verse 23). Do you ever waver in your faith? I do sometimes. I'll be the first to admit it. And how is it that we are to keep holding fast the confession of our hope without wavering? Notice the phrase **"let us."** We need to do it *together.* We can't do it on our own.

At the same time **"let us consider how to stimulate one another to love and good deeds"** (verse 24). *Love and good deeds* is a summary of the Great Commandment in Matthew 22:37–39: **"You shall love the Lord your God with all your heart . . . [and] you shall love your neighbor as yourself."** It's all there.

Have you ever blown on a fire when the coals were dying down? Dads love to show off their powerful lungs with that campfire move. You blow all the embers off the coals, and then *poof*, a new flame comes up. In the body of Christ, we are supposed to be doing that for each other. Sometimes sin or doubt or just the film of life itself puts a thick coating of soot on our lives, which makes it hard to connect with God. What we desperately need is for a loving brother or sister to come along and blow off the embers. That's the idea behind the word *stimulate*. We are supposed to be fanning the flames of love and good works in each other's lives. In the church, we stimulate each other to greater passion for God.

In our church, that happens in small groups—little groups of people who gather together for Bible study, prayer, encouragement, and accountability. Maybe in your church, that happens in a Sunday school class or some other format. The form is not important, but the function is essential. Every man needs brothers who are challenging him to be all he can be under God for his family. Every wife needs sisters in the Lord who are calling her to be a woman of virtue and a wife who makes her marriage stronger in the Lord. Do you have people like that in your life? The place to find them is at church.

Often I speak with believers who are wondering, "Why do I seem to be losing? Other people are just racing ahead spiritually, but I'm just going along for a ride." I am telling you why right now. It takes more than a weekend worship experience with God. It takes meaningful connectedness with the followers of Jesus Christ, believers getting together and challenging one another and exhorting one another. When that is happening for you on a regular basis, the blessings that flow into your family will be immense and immediate.

DO NOT FORSAKE BUT ENCOURAGE

Third, we are to be encouraging when we come together: **"Not forsaking our own assembling together, as is the habit of some, but encouraging one another"** (verse 25). The church of Jesus Christ isn't like a Target store. It's not like you go, get what you came for, and then head home again. The church isn't just about you getting what you need. It's about you participating in what *everyone* needs. It is a community of families all working together so that the church can be all God wants it to be. When you finally cross over and become a giver and not just a receiver, then you will see your faith really flourish and grow. When you pick up your responsibility to encourage others in the church, God will bless and prosper your own family.

In our church, I talk to people for twenty to thirty minutes after every service. Often people will come to complain about their old church or sometimes ours. I've found that nine of every ten people who are dissatisfied with their church are not participating in it. They are not worshiping regularly or fervently, they are not connected in meaningful relationships with others, and they have never rolled up their sleeves to get involved. If your church believes the Bible and teaches it, I guarantee you will get a lot more benefit out of it for your family if you participate.

Notice the end of verse 25, **"And all the more as you see the day drawing near."** The idea there is that you don't know how many more times you'll get to go to church. You say, "Man! You are really turning the screws on me to worship Christ and walk with Christ and work for Christ! You are *turning* the screws!" Yes, and let me do so with joy and not with grief, for that would be unprofitable for you! OK? Nothing would bring me greater joy than knowing that you had taken this chapter to heart and recommitted yourself to full participation in the church of Jesus Christ. God's Word teaches that local churches are to be independent and self-governing, but it does not teach the autonomy of the local believer.

If you have been trying to go it alone, I urge you in the name of the Lord Jesus to get back to the church. It's where the action is. It's where your family will grow and flourish in the Lord. Go for it!

A PRAYER TO GO HIGHER

Lord, thank You for loving the church and giving Yourself for her. Forgive me, Lord, for being disillusioned by the very thing to which You are so committed. Forgive me for not being what I need to be in Your church. Thank You for my own local church, just one of the many places where You are working throughout the world. Just one expression of the body of Christ. Thank You for the people that are there. Thank You, Lord, for the gifts that are there.

Lord, help me to recognize the church as the incredible resource that it is for my family—to help me to be a better parent, to make my marriage stronger, to bring me into accountable relationships where I can be committed to doing the things that I know are right. Help me to step forward into more meaningful connectedness to this glorious thing, Your church. We are Your bride. We are living stones. We are a royal priesthood. Lord, build Your church through me and my family, and bring glory to Yourself through it.

These things I pray in the strong and precious name of Jesus. Amen.

A PROJECT TO GO DEEPER

Two of the best New Testament depictions of the church are found in Acts 2:42–47 and 1 Corinthians 12:12–27. Read and meditate upon these passages, and journal some of your thoughts and impressions. How does your local church compare to these pictures? Does your church involvement match up with what's described in these texts? What could you do to more closely reflect the intent of these verses?

A PRACTICE TO GO FURTHER

Keep in mind that it's not enough to simply hear God's Word, or even to meditate upon it—we must *act* upon it! Choose at least one action step from your reflection above, and go to work. Take some step to demonstrate your belief in, submission to, and participation in the local church. It could be that you need to join a small group or some other smaller gathering of believers. Maybe you want to be an usher and help greet those who come to your church. Perhaps you sense the Lord leading you to get involved with the youth ministry. Maybe you want to begin praying very regularly and specifically for your pastor and church leaders.

Whatever it is, do it with all your might (see Colossians 3:23).

CHAPTER SEVEN

WORD #6:
COMMITMENT

⇥ ⇤

E xcellent effort on your part! The vast majority of readers do not make it this far, even in the very best of books. If you choose to finish what you start, you reveal that you have some of what this chapter deals with—something that very few families seem to have these days. The word is *commitment,* and God will bring blessing and transformation to your family through this word like almost no other.

In Joshua 24, Joshua had led the children of Israel right up to the edge of the Promised Land. The people were like, "Are we going in or aren't we? Are we going to get the blessings of God or aren't we?" Joshua laid it all on the line: "**Now, therefore, fear the Lord and serve Him in sincerity and truth; and put away the gods which your fathers served beyond the River and in Egypt, . . . choose for yourselves today whom you will serve . . . but as for me and my house, we will serve the Lord**" (verses 14–15). No wandering, no waffling, no wavering back and forth. Just make a choice, take a stand, buckle down, and commit.

Perception is not reality. You may have perceptions about why certain families are fulfilled and harmonious, but the realities of why these families "work" may be very different than how it appears. I was with a man recently who made that point clear for me. He said, "James, you're a pastor, so you must know the Bible." I said, "Well, yes, I have spent a lot of time studying God's Word."

Then he quickly asked, "In what numerical groupings did Moses take the animals on the ark?" "Two by two," I shot back. "Moses didn't take *any* animals on the ark! It was Noah." I was like, "Oh, I can't believe I blew that! The people in my church would be so embarrassed."

He said, "I'll give you another chance, James. Really concentrate, OK? Now spell the word *silk*." I was nervous, so very slowly I said, "S . . . I . . . L . . . K." As soon as I was finished, he said, "What do cows drink?" I was like, "Milk!" He said, "No, they *make* milk. They don't drink it!" I couldn't believe he took me again. Perception is not reality.

Often we think that what we see in families, what we perceive as the reasons for their success, are in fact the realities—but they are not. You look at some families and say to yourself, "I know what they have going on. That couple has great chemistry. If we just had chemistry like they have, we would have the marriage they have." You look at other families and say to yourself, "Look at their parents. Look at their grandparents. What a background!" You consider these factors and say, "*That's* the thing that makes for a successful, happy, God-honoring family." Listen: perception is not reality. Every family that you respect and admire has its own set of problems.

But at the center of an ever-successful family is a rock-solid commitment. Guaranteed, they have developed an unswerving, unalterable, unending commitment to do life together under God. Let's study some teaching Jesus did on commitment and examine how He interacted with people who claimed to be committed—but were not.

GET OFF THE FENCE.

Jesus once told a large crowd: **"If anyone comes to Me, and does not hate his own father and mother and wife and children and brothers and sisters, yes, and even his own life, he cannot be My disciple"** (Luke 14:26). Anything less than total, 100 percent, radical commitment to Christ is not commitment at all. You say, "What does He mean by *hate* my father and mother?" In Matthew 10, Jesus said it a different way to his twelve disciples: **"He who loves father or mother more than Me is not worthy of Me; and he who loves son or daughter more than Me is not worthy of Me"** (verse 37). That's what commitment is—to put Christ above everything. Above my family. Above my spouse. Above my children. Above everything.

As the parents of three wonderful children, Kathy and I have talked about the tension we feel with this truth. We love our kids so much that it is difficult at times not to feel like we are in danger of loving them more than we love God. But we have come to see that to allow our kids to mean more to us than our relationship with the Lord is to put them in great danger. In fact, isn't that the whole point of God's actions toward Abraham and Isaac? God told Abraham, "You can't love anyone or anything more than Me, so get your son and take him up on the mountain and offer him on an altar there." You can check out Genesis 22 for the full story. The test was on.

A couple of summers ago, when our family was overseas on sabbatical, I was wrestling with this exact thing. I was spending every day with our kids, and I felt myself becoming attached to them in a way that was hindering my walk with the Lord. Many mornings that summer, I prayed and wrestled with the tension of allowing my family to mean more to me than God. We talked about it, prayed about it, and then I made a decision.

In a northern section of England known as the Lake District, on two separate days I took each of my sons (our daughter was still too young then) and walked for several miles to the top of a high hill. We could see for miles. Everywhere we looked were green pastures, stone fences, and little groupings of sheep. The town of Coniston was just a speck in the distance beneath the low-hanging clouds. The surroundings were beautiful. There in that place, I sat on a rock with each of my sons and opened my Bible. I read to each the story of Abraham and Isaac and tried my best to explain: "Son, I cannot allow myself to ever love you more than I love God." We discussed what that meant and knelt together. I laid my hands on them and consecrated myself before the Lord that they would never eclipse my commitment to Christ.

In many ways, your family also must come to grips with what it means for God to be your first and highest commitment. Anything less is not commitment at all. However, when God is in His rightful place, then that same kind of commitment can flow down to your family. When it does, incredible blessing will follow.

A Dangerous Approach

Recently, I had lunch with a man in our church who I knew was seriously dating one of our finest young ladies. I had heard they were considering marriage, so I was excited for a chance to talk with him and learn a little bit about his view of commitment. Well, to say the least, I was very shocked when he told me that they were having struggles over his ongoing relationships with former girlfriends. "She's so insecure," he said. "She just can't accept the fact that I want to check in with my old girlfriends from time to time and see how they're doing. Nothing official, just a dinner out or whatever. I cannot understand what's wrong with her."

"I can't understand what's wrong with *you!*" I replied. "She understands a lot more about commitment than you do. Don't you understand that lifetime love is exclusive, that it's a complete commitment to one person? For a lifetime! You don't have eyes for anyone but that single woman. Absolute, total commitment." Later I told the young woman to lose the guy if he didn't figure this out, but by God's grace it appears that he got the message.

Anything less than total commitment does not produce the power necessary to defeat your enemies, deliver your priorities, and destroy your obstacles. That's the kind of commitment God uses to bless our relationship with Him, and that's the kind of commitment God uses to make our family relationships all He desires them to be.

CALCULATE THE COST.

You say, "That's pretty hard. Total commitment to my family will not come without a price." You're right, so let's make sure that the cost of our commitment has been calculated. In Luke 14:27, Jesus declared, "**Whoever does not carry his own cross and come after Me cannot be My disciple.**" The cross in this verse is symbolic of the hardships related to following Christ. What are some of these hardships? For starters, life is a daily grind and every day you have to stay at it. Another cross we must pick up is the rejection that comes with following the Lord. As you begin to live the radical commitment Jesus calls for, there are some people who are like, "Forget you!" and you need to be willing to say, "OK, forget me because I am all about following Jesus Christ." Then there is the cross of having a new Master and living for Him, rather than for yourself. Remaining faithful to Christ, even through difficult circumstances, is a cross that every believer must carry.

Many other examples could be given to prove that picking up my cross and carrying it every day is not an easy life, but it is the only true Christian life. If I refuse to carry my cross daily, I cannot be Christ's disciple.

Then in verse 28, Jesus gave an illustration: **"For which one of you, when he wants to build a tower"**—I don't build towers, but I think I get the idea—**"does not first sit down and calculate the cost to see if he has enough to complete it?"** The word *calculate* means literally *pebble*. It was used in reference to a one-by-one count: "Well, this tower is going to take two hundred twenty-nine thousand four hundred seventy-eight bricks. And it's going to take thirty-seven thousand three hundred twenty-three pieces of steel. Do we have that much on hand?" That's the kind of measuring Jesus calls for when we are calculating what it will take to keep our commitments.

Can I finish the course? Can I follow Christ to the end? Can I be a faithful husband for my whole life? Can I be the wife God has called me to be? Am I willing to pay the price of godly parenting? If I am unwilling, I have no business making the commitment in the first place. Remember, commitment is powerful when the cost is calculated. You walk to the front of the church like I did almost eighteen years ago, and you stand there with someone and say, "To have and to hold from this day forward, for better, for worse, for richer, for poorer, in sickness and in health, and forsaking all others, I give myself only to you as long as we both shall live." Now that is a huge commitment! You have to count the cost of that commitment ahead of time.

COMMITMENT IS THE DEFINING CHARACTERISTIC OF LIFE.

A man I greatly respect said, "Commitment is the defining characteristic of a person's life." How true! There are people who keep their commitments, and there are people who don't. It's the watershed issue. Which person are you? What kind of family do you have? Do you keep the commitments you make?

Some of the families in our church recently went to a marriage conference called "I *Still* Do." What a phenomenal name for a marriage conference! It's not just, "I do." Any guy can walk to the front of the church and say, "I do. C'mon. Let's go to Hawaii." But to stand there ten, twenty, thirty, forty, even fifty years later and say, "I *still* do"—there is power in that! It is power that will flow down into the lives of your children and into your grandchildren. Commitment is a powerful tool for family transformation when the cost is calculated.

FINISH THE COURSE.

Back to the tower thing again. Jesus continued: **"Otherwise, when he has laid a foundation and is not able to finish, all who observe it begin to ridicule him"** (Luke 14:29). The word *ridicule* there means *to mock* or literally *to play with a child*. "Billy, you couldn't finish your tower. Your eyes are bigger than your wallet. You silly dumb-dumb. You tried to do more than you can handle." Isn't that exactly what happens? You make a commitment to Jesus Christ and go public with it, and then your family is like, "Set the clock. It's just a phase she is going through. She'll come around. . . . He will come to his senses." Isn't that right? First John 2:19 says, **"They went out from us, but they were not really of us; for if they had been of us, they would have remained with us; but they went out, so that it would be shown that they all are not of us."** It is enduring to the end that proves the legitimacy of a profession of faith.

Jesus Christ is very interested in us finishing what we start. He is looking for finishers in a world of quitters. Did you know that five thousand babies are abandoned annually in the United States? Quitters! Almost 30 percent of American kids live in single-parent homes—to say nothing of the second-parent homes or the countless kids who come home to empty houses where money is more important than children. This is failure to finish to the very end what we begin. Commitment is a powerful tool for family transformation.

Successful parenting is not simply getting your kids through high school or college. It just grieves me so much when people say, "Just a couple more years and our kids will be grown and gone." What are they talking about? Parenting is a job for a hundred years. That's how long it lasts—an entire century!

You say, "I don't think I'm even going to be around for a hundred years." No, but your children and your grandchildren will be. Descendants of yours whom you will never lay eyes upon or have a single conversation with, but they'll know you! They'll know the kind of life you lived. They'll know the kind of opportunity you've given them. They'll know whether or not you were a person who kept your commitments.

Ray Stedman, who is now with the Lord, was for many years the pastor of Peninsula Bible Church outside San Francisco. I respected him so much. He observed this:

I've been in homes where there is no testimony to God or recognition of him at all. And yet they have been orderly homes, moral homes, loving homes—a joy to be in—and where the children are . . . able to cope with life. Some people are ready to say, "What difference, then, does Christianity add?"

The answer is that if you investigate a home like that you will find that just a generation or so back there has been significant Christian exposure somewhere in that family. In other words, secular homes of that character are living on the capital of faith which has been invested by a previous generation."[1]

Wow! What we do affects our children. It affects our grandchildren. Anybody can start something. That's nothing. The world is filled with starters. Up like a rocket and down like a rock. The power of commitment is released into your family when you determine that under all circumstances, you will finish what you start.

PAY THE PRICE.

Perhaps you're thinking, *Well, if commitment is such a great thing, why don't more people have it?* That's a great question, and the answer is seen in Jesus' final illustration on commitment from Luke 14:31: **"Or what king, when he sets out to meet another king in battle, will not first sit down and consider whether he is strong enough with ten thousand men to encounter the one coming against him with twenty thousand?"**

The report comes in, "Hey, King! There are twenty thousand soldiers marching on our city!" The king asks, "How many do we have?" "Ten thousand." The king is like, "OK, but are we stronger?" And he begins to count the cost and determine if he is willing to pay the price. "Can we win? How many casualties will there be? Are we willing to live with the consequences of what we are committing to?"

Verse 32: **"Or else, while the other is still far away, he sends a delegation and asks for terms of peace."** If you can't win, stay out of the battle. The bottom line is this: Kings who defend their kingdoms only until hardship comes or suffering is required or a price must be paid—they don't have their kingdoms very long. Similarly, people who follow Christ only until someone rejects them for their faith, or their integrity costs them their job, or they become weary of the pursuit of holiness—they don't follow Christ very long.

Families that stay together and keep growing only until difficulties come or conflicts arise or a price must be paid—they never become all that God would have them be and never experience the joy of successful family living.

Chris Spielman, the former middle linebacker for the Buffalo Bills, is a man who knows and has seen the benefits of this kind of lesson. If you follow football at all, you know that this guy was as tough as they come. He was fast and aggressive and refused to back down from anybody on the field. During the 1995 season, he had a tear in his pectoral muscle, but he steadfastly refused to sit out a game. He played the entire season with excruciating pain because he didn't want to let his teammates down. Then in 1998, he appeared to reverse field and sat out the whole season—never made a tackle, never showed up for a game—because his wife had breast cancer. When she was going through the pain of chemotherapy, he was there every step of the way supporting her. When she was sick to her stomach from the treatments, he was right by her side. Through the tests and the surgery, through the pain and uncertainty, he put his entire career on hold to focus on his marriage.

The newspapers and others were challenging him, "How could you let your teammates down? They need you, but you're refusing to play." Spielman explained he had a higher priority, saying, "What kind of man would I be if I backed out of my word to her? I wouldn't be a man at all."[2]

He was right. That's the power of commitment. Absolute, total commitment. Even when a price has to be paid.

WHY DO FAMILIES BREAK THEIR COMMITMENTS?

You say, "I want a family like that. I want that kind of commitment for my home. I can see the power of it. But why is it so hard to be committed?" Let's consider that for a moment. Why do families break their commitments? Why do husbands and wives walk out on each other? Twenty-one percent of men and 11 percent of women *admit* to infidelity in their marriage. Why do children disown their parents and vice versa? And how about the hundreds of little broken commitments: "I'll be home by 6:00 P.M. for sure!" or, "Yes, I'll be at your next game, Son. I promise!" Then it's not done. Why do families break their commitments? From Luke 9, here are three reasons. I think you'll recognize them.

REASON #1: COST NOT COUNTED AHEAD OF TIME

Luke reported, "**As they were going along the road, someone said to Him, 'I will follow you wherever You go'**" (9:57). That sounds pretty good, doesn't it? "Hey, Jesus! I'll follow You wherever You go!" On one level, you have to respect the guy. After all, he has his *job* right: "I am going to be following. I don't have any maps. I don't have any plans. I don't have any ideas. I don't have any agendas. I am going to be on Your program, Lord." He also has the *roles* right: "You're the boss; I am the employee. I am going to be the follower; You are going to be the leader." And then he has the *extent* right: "I will follow You wherever You go—hills, valleys, cities, countries, highs, lows, good times, bad times." If a guy like that shows up at the average church, they're like, "Sign him up!" And he will be up giving his testimony in three weeks.

But notice Jesus' response in verse 58: "**The foxes have holes and the birds of the air have nests, but the Son of Man has nowhere to lay His head.**" He was saying, "Dude, you don't know what you're talking about. You haven't counted the cost. Are you going to follow Me wherever I go? Do you know where I go? Did you know that I don't even have a place to sleep at night?" The man had expressed such a strong desire to be committed, but he had not counted the cost. And Christ rejected him.

Maybe you are at a place right now where your commitment to your family is costing you a lot. Maybe your marriage is taking a lot more energy than it has at other times. Maybe you are carrying a heavy burden for one of your children, and you are wondering if keeping your commitment is really worth all that it is costing you. Don't give up! The power that comes on the other side of commitment is incredible, but the pain of breaking your family commitments is something from which few people ever recover.

The other week I read an article that Chuck Swindoll had clipped from the *Los Angeles Times* about a man named David Berg. This man walked into the hospital looking like an advertisement for a health club. He was twenty-two years old, 6 feet 4 inches tall, and weighed two hundred five pounds. He had been running and working out daily with weights. In just a month, he was scheduled to begin his senior year at the University of South Dakota, where he was an honor student in the field of biology. He wanted to become a veterinarian. The last few days of his summer vacation, he planned an elective

143

surgery at the hospital to take care of a nagging groin problem. It was considered such a routine procedure that the doctor told him, "Don't worry! You'll be camping again in no time." He had planned a trip for two weeks later, but he never made it.

> These days, David Berg lies in a hospital room in Inglewood, California, looking pale and fragile. At one hundred twenty-five pounds, he is so weak that he can no longer sit up in bed. Heavily sedated to control muscle spasms, Berg lies flat on his back and gazes with seemingly frightened blue eyes at a world his neurologist says is only a blur to him. . . .
>
> Every six hours, a nurse interrupts the monotony by connecting a thin, plastic tube to an opening in his stomach so that he can be fed some liquid. When he soils his diapers, he must lie in them until a nurse comes because he is mute and can communicate only by small gestures such as blinking his eyes. . . . An error in administering an anesthetic deprived Berg of oxygen for about twenty minutes and left him with severe brain damage.[3]

At the age of sixty-three, his father gave up his Brentwood law practice to take care of David, and he is the most frequent visitor in the hospital. David's father

> said that unlike someone in a coma, his son is worse off because he is fully aware of his plight. He added that for a parent the death of a child would be easier to take. "With death comes finality, and the memory grows dimmer. The essence of this tragedy is a continuing one. It goes on and on and on."[4]

None of us knows what is around the corner. You may have something very difficult drop out of nowhere and severely test your family's commitment. You may be called upon to do something that in this moment you can't imagine, like David's father surrendering his career to help his ailing son. Or maybe you're already in that kind of crucible. Don't give up. Keep pressing on one day at a time, or if need be, one step at a time. It's when you want most to throw in the towel that you simply must press in and push forward, drawing upon the Lord's strength to keep the commitments you have made to your family.

There is power in that! The families that you respect, the ones you see that seem to be doing so well—they have this; I guarantee it. And you can have it, too. But don't kid yourself. There is a cost that must be counted ahead of time.

REASON #2: PRICE NOT PAID DURING HARDSHIP

Why do families break their commitment? A second reason is because the price is not paid during hardship. Look at Luke 9:59–60. This time the invitation comes from Jesus: **"He said to another, 'Follow Me.' But he [answered], 'Lord, permit me first to go and bury my father.' But He said to him, 'Allow the dead to bury their own dead; but as for you, go and proclaim everywhere the kingdom of God.'"** That seems like a reasonable request: "Let me go bury my father, and then I am with You." For Jewish people, the burial of a family member was the supreme duty. Rabbis were permitted to be absent at worship even on holy days to bury a family member. However, Christ is not questioning the reasonableness of his request.

The reason Jesus rejects this man as a committed disciple is because of his first four words: **"Lord, permit me first."** Those words are an oxymoron. (An oxymoron is two things that don't go together.) It's like *pennant-winning Chicago Cubs* or *Canadian military*. (Since I'm a Canadian who roots for the Cubs, those examples hurt to admit!) "Lord, me first" just doesn't work. Even the greatest of human obligations must not compete with allegiance to Christ. In a similar way, no human activity or responsibility should interfere with my family: not work, not leisure, not friends, not education.

You say, "Wow, that's a high price!" Yes, it is. But the failure to pay the price will bring absolute devastation to your family. Think of a person like Dennis Rodman or Howard Stern. If you don't know who those people are, I am not going to parade their perversity before you. Let me just say that they are two of the sickest and most distorted people in the entertainment world! We tend to think, *Well, they just* became *like that*. No, not true. Pull the thread back to their beginning and you find broken family commitments.

Dennis Rodman has not seen his father for thirty years because his father lives in the Philippines with two different wives and their fifteen children. In various interviews over the years, Rodman's father has bragged of fathering a total of twenty-seven children, and according to a recent statement in *Newsweek*, he said that his life goal is to father thirty. Yet he hasn't seen even one of these children for thirty years![5] The perversity of his son Dennis is apparent to those who follow the former NBA star, but we should not be surprised to discover that it is rooted in broken hearts from broken family commitments.

In an interview with *Rolling Stone* magazine, Howard Stern briefly and unusually let down his guard and said, "I will never have a lot of self-esteem. I don't feel very good about myself. The way I was raised, my father was always telling me that I was a piece of (expletive). I think I'll go to my grave not feeling very good about myself or that I am special in any way. My mother used to tell me that I was special. But every time I would hear my mother's voice saying, 'You are a special little boy,' I would hear my father saying, 'You (expletive)! You are nothing but a piece of (expletive)!'"[6]

It's not always easy to be a father. It's not always easy to be a mother. It's not always easy to be a faithful spouse. But the price must be paid, even during hardship. If not, the commitment will break down.

REASON #3: COURSE NOT FINISHED

This is a third reason why families break their commitments. Look at Luke 9:61–62: **"Another also said, 'I will follow You, Lord; but first permit me'**—there it is again!—**'to say good-bye to those at home.' But Jesus said to him, 'No one, after putting his hand to the plow and looking back, is fit for the kingdom of God.'"** That is commitment in God's kingdom. Keep your hand on the plow. We are not looking back. We are not going backward. This is what we committed ourselves to do, and we are going to keep on doing it for the rest of our lives.

Maybe the big issue for you is not divorce or estrangement or abandonment. Perhaps the issue at your house is that you fly off the handle, and you never apologize or make things right. Maybe you don't know how to say you're sorry. Perhaps you are so consumed with work or distracted by other things that you don't focus in on your son or daughter. Maybe you neglect your marriage and don't give your spouse the emotional nourishment he or she longs for. What is your problem? You signed up for life. Finish the course!

HOW CAN I SHARPEN MY FAMILY COMMITMENT?

You say, "I want an upgrade. How do I sharpen my family commitment?" Here are four words to help you improve the commitment in your family.

CONSECRATE

First, consecrate your family. The word *consecrate* means *to declare holy or to set apart for the worship of God*. Maybe you should start repenting of a halfhearted, shallow commitment to your family. Repent of selfishness and distractedness and avoidance of your number one responsibility under God— your family. Go to some of your family members and ask for forgiveness. Be specific. Say, "I'm sorry. I haven't been the mother God wants be to me. I have been distracted by other things." Or, "I haven't been the husband God wants me to be. Please forgive me." Don't be ashamed to acknowledge before your family that God is dealing with your heart.

Things can be different. God wants them to be different. It can start with *you*. Consecrate.

COMMUNICATE

Second, share with your family a vision of commitment. Gather your whole family together and say, "Hey, we are the _____ (fill in your own family name). We keep our commitments." It's not always easy to do: "No, Son, you can't quit the football team. I'm sorry it is hard for you right now. You don't have to play next year, but we gave our word we would follow through. We don't quit stuff. I know Billy quits. That's *their* family. This is *our* family." Give your family a vision of absolute, total commitment. Here would be a great thing just to say to each other: "Absolute, total commitment— ATC. That's what we're all about. ATC. You don't ever have to worry if Mom and Dad are going to be around. We are going to be around! You don't ever have to worry if you hear us fighting that we are not going to work it out because we are going to work it out! We are in this for life!"

Speak that vision over your family, and watch the transforming power of God begin to build in your home. Communicate.

COOPERATE

Third, the family must learn to cooperate. A big part of commitment is give-and-take, isn't it? I can't always have my way. I can't do everything I want to do—not if I want to have the family of my dreams. You can't have your cake and eat it, too. Sometimes, you have to give in.

"OK, I'll stay home tonight. You go out." "Yeah, I'll come home a little bit early." "OK, I won't do that on Saturday. We need to do some family things. No problem. This comes first." Cooperate.

CHRIST

Lastly, and so importantly, Christ is vital in the process of sharpening your family's commitment. This is definitely one of those "don't-try-this-at-home" messages. If you think this is some sort of pep talk on commitment, it isn't. You do not have within yourself the strength to do what I am talking about doing. If it doesn't emerge from a personal intimacy with Christ, if it doesn't emerge from a complete surrender under His lordship, it will never happen.

Maybe in this moment you are sensing, "O God, I am not proud of everything that has been. I am not proud of everything that I have said and done." But here is the marvelous news of the grace of God. It matters not what *has been;* what matters is what *can be.* By God's grace you can be a person of commitment.

A PRAYER TO GO HIGHER

Lord, give my family a fresh infusion of Your grace and Your love. God, forgive me for allowing other things to eclipse the eternal responsibility of leading and shepherding my family. Give me faith to see the power that is in commitment. Help me, Lord. I need Your strength to obey Your Word and apply these truths.

Show me the areas that I can work on in my own life. Reveal to me how I can be better for my family. Lord, don't let me just go through the motions, but might this truth change me and grow me into all that You desire for me to be. Teach me, I pray, the power of commitment. I ask these things in the precious name of Your Son, Jesus Christ. Amen.

A PROJECT TO GO DEEPER

Paul said in Philippians, "**Do nothing from selfishness or empty conceit, but with humility of mind regard one another as more important than yourselves; do not merely look out for your own personal interests, but also for the interests of others**" (2:3–4). How do "selfishness" and "personal interests" impact commitment in a family between spouses, between parents and children, and among siblings? How have you seen this in your own family relationships? On the other hand, what effect does acting "with humility of mind" have on the level of commitment in a family? Can you recall any personal examples of this?

A PRACTICE TO GO FURTHER

The people who know you best know whether you truly are a committed person. Do you want to hear what they think? If you feel like you need to step up your commitment in your family, sit down and talk with some of the people who know you best and ask them for their advice. Interview your spouse, your parents, your children, your siblings, your closest friend. Ask them to honestly evaluate your current commitment level and to offer some practical suggestions for your improvement. Take the best two or three ideas and begin to work on them right away.

NOTES

1. Ray Stedman et. al., *Family Life* (Waco, Tex.: Word, 1973), 56–57.
2. Rob Bentz, "A Linebacker's Tough Choice," *Men of Integrity*, 15 January 2001.
3. Ralph Cipriano, "Downey Man Brain-Damaged During Routine Surgery, Huge Payment Can't Erase Medical Tragedy," *Los Angeles Times*, 1–2 June 1985, 1, 3; as quoted in Charles R. Swindoll, *Growing Wise in Family Life* (Portland, Ore.: Multnomah, 1988), 233–234.
4. Ibid., 234.
5. "Perspectives," *Newsweek*, 9 September 1996, 25; as cited in Steve Farrar, *Anchor Man* (Nashville: Nelson, 1998), 1–2.
6. R. Marin, "Interview with Howard Stern," *Rolling Stone*, 10 February 1994, 28 ff.; as quoted in Steve Farrar, *Anchor Man*, 2.

PART 3:
ONE
TRANSFORMING
WORD

>>> <<<

7. Love

WORD #7:
LOVE

→≫ ≪←

Well, you're nearly at the finish line, but this is not the time to stop. Our final word is the very air that transformed families breathe. It is the soil in which the previous six words can germinate and grow. The word is *love*. Without love, our pursuit of transformation will grate on our families and cause strife. But with love, our energies can soothe, even when the road to change is not smooth.

Love is a popular word in our world today, yet for the most part, it is misunderstood and misused. Still, *love* is a powerful word; most importantly, it's a biblical word. Scripture has so much to say about the transforming power of love, and about what it can do for a broken marriage, a severed relationship, or a struggling family. The Scriptures tell us:

- *Love is a family debt worth having.* "**Owe nothing to anyone except to love one another**" (Romans 13:8).
- *Love keeps our families thinking clear.* "**If we are of sound mind, it is . . . the love of Christ [that] controls us**" (2 Corinthians 5:13–14).
- *Love fuels family harmony.* "**Walk . . . with all humility and gentleness, with patience, showing tolerance for one another in love**" (Ephesians 4:1–2).

- *Love binds our families together.* "Their hearts . . . [have] been knit together in love" (Colossians 2:2).
- *Love keeps us from focusing on family failures.* "Keep fervent in your love for one another, because love covers a multitude of sins" (1 Peter 4:8).
- *God's love allows us to conquer every family obstacle.* "In all these things we overwhelmingly conquer through Him who loved us" (Romans 8:37).

It's no wonder, then, that 1 Corinthians 13:13 says that *love is the greatest thing:* "But now faith, hope, love, abide these three; but the greatest of these is love."

WHAT'S BETTER THAN LOVE?

Isn't it strange that many people, as they think about fixing and adjusting and growing and changing their family, don't consider love? Actually, 1 Corinthians 13 highlights five things people think can do more to change their family than love:

1. TALK

Verse 1 says, "If I speak with the tongues of men and of angels, but do not have love, I have become a noisy gong or a clanging cymbal." A lot of people don't believe that. They think *talk* will change their family. "We are going to sit down and have a talk. I know some things that you don't, and you're going to hear them right now. We have to talk about this. We have to blah, blah, blah about that." And on and on it goes. Now, I am all for families talking things through, but if your words are not backed up by love, it doesn't matter how eloquent you are or how clear you can make things.

Communication that is not rooted in love is not only fruitless; it is counterproductive to the things God wants to do in your family.

2. KNOWLEDGE

Knowledge is another thing people think can bring more family transformation than love. Notice in verse 2, "If I have the gift of prophecy, and know

all mysteries and all knowledge." Send your kid to a good school—a seminary, in fact—and have him learn everything there is to know about God. Or encourage him to get good grades and earn a scholarship to a major university. We can train our kids to think like Einstein and write like a Pulitzer Prize-winning author, but without love, it amounts to nothing.

It's no secret that I'm a "truth guy." I am fired up about knowing the truth, telling the truth, and living the truth. Jesus Himself said, **"The truth will make you free"** (John 8:32). But free for what? Free to love God! Free to love others. Free to love my family. If the truth doesn't yield a greater harvest of love in my life and in my family, it is useless.

3. FAITH

Some people think *faith* can do more than love for their family. Verse 2 continues, **"And if I have all faith, so as to remove mountains."** Now that is big-time faith! Faith is important, no doubt about it. Hebrews 11:6 teaches that it is impossible to please God without faith. But you can have all the faith in the world, and if you don't have love, you have a big bag of zilch.

When I was growing up, I knew some parents who thought it was all about faith. They force-fed their faith to their kids and forgot about love. Sadly, many of those kids are out of church and in the world today. It doesn't take a kid very long to start asking, "If having faith in God is such a great thing, if it makes your life so much better, then why doesn't your life show it?" Most children figure out that parents who don't love don't have a real thing with God. Faith can't exist by itself; it has to be rooted in love.

4. COMPASSION

You say, "Well, we are a really *compassionate* family. We feed the poor. We help out at the Rotary Club and give our extra clothing to Goodwill." Notice in verse 3: **"If I give all my possessions to feed the poor . . . but do not have love, it profits me nothing."** Not even feeding the poor, not even supporting single parents, not even sending dollars to Africa will have an impact on your family if there is a lack of love at home.

Compassion alone will not change your family.

5. SACRIFICE

Some people think that *sacrifice* is more important than love. They say, "I am giving everything for my family. Do you know how many hours I work each week? Do you have any idea the way I am spending myself for my kids? Do you realize the effort that I am expending to make sure my family has the best of opportunities in this world?" But notice in verse 3: **"If I surrender my body to be burned, but do not have love, it profits me nothing."** That's a reference to martyrdom in the early church. Even if I were to literally give up my *life* for my family, but I didn't love them, or they didn't know that I loved them, it would be worthless.

I'm telling you, love is the greatest thing.

LOVE IS POWERFUL.

That's why 1 Corinthians 13:8 says, **"Love never fails."** Forget that you've heard it before, and hear it again for the first time. Love never fails! Never! You say, "Love never fails to do what?" It never fails to do anything! Love never fails to win back the heart of a distant loved one that has grown cold and hard. Love never fails to conquer years of neglect. Love never fails to bring a stubborn, willful child back into the fold.

Whatever burden you have for your family—if you want to cooperate with God in what He is trying to do—get hold of this thing called love. Love is powerful. Love never fails.

LOVE IS PROTECTION.

Love is also protection. Consider 1 John 3:11: **"For this is the message which you have heard from the beginning, that we should love one another."** Notice that this message is not a new one. It's just the same stuff that Jesus had told His disciples in John 13:34–35: **"A new commandment I give to you, that you love one another, even as I have loved you. . . . By this all men will know that you are My disciples, if you have love for one another."** You see, John was there when Jesus first spoke those words. He is like, "This isn't new stuff."

Yet so many people today are saying, "I have this new thing. I figured it out. This is what every family needs." They're writing books like *The Five*

Strategic This and *The New Keys to That*. God has already told us what the most important thing is, and it's not new. In fact, I've heard it said, "If it's new, it's not true; and if it's true, it's not new." Or as King Solomon put it, "**There is nothing new under the sun**" (Ecclesiastes 1:9). We don't need anything new because we already have the thing that Jesus gave. "**For this is the message which you have heard from the beginning, that we should love one another**" (1 John 3:11). That's the "new" program. Love one another.

A GRAPHIC ILLUSTRATION

Biblical love is protecting love. John gives a graphic illustration of what happens when we abandon protecting love: "**We should love one another; not as Cain, who was of the evil one and slew his brother**" (1 John 3:11–12). You remember Cain, don't you? He was the son of Adam and Eve—the firstborn son who killed his brother, Abel. In fact, the word *slew* there means literally *cut his throat*. Cain brutally murdered his younger brother.

You say, "Why would he do something like that? Why would a person kill a member of his family?" Well, sad but true, people do it both literally and figuratively all the time. While it's only the literal murders that you hear about in the papers, people all around us are dying in their families!

As a pastor, I regularly hear stories about families that are divided and fighting over the estate of their parents. And then there are the children who are tearing their families apart through rebellion. Why do people do stuff like that? The answer is right there in 1 John 3:12: "**And for what reason did [Cain] slay him? Because his deeds were evil, and his brother's were righteous.**" Never underestimate the conflict that rages in the heart of a person who is in the process of rejecting God. Never underestimate the tension that person feels between your life and theirs. Look at verse 13, "**Do not be surprised, brethren, if the world hates you.**" The word *world* there refers to the people you know: your neighbors, your coworkers, your family members who have not received Christ and are not walking in Him.

THE SATANIC SOURCE OF FAMILY CONFLICT

Notice where the text goes from there. It gives not only the reason why a person would do such things—"**because his deeds were evil, and his brother's** were righteous" and because "**men loved the darkness rather than the Light**" (John 3:19)—but also the *source* of this evil, this conflict. "**Not as Cain, who was of the evil one.**" All evil in our world is rooted ultimately in the father of evil, Satan himself. Satan, the one who shattered the first family in history through his influence over Cain, has the very same goal today: to shatter your family. And he is working on it.

Peter warned his readers, "**Your adversary, the devil, prowls around like a roaring lion, seeking someone to devour**" (1 Peter 5:8). Some people, through their own disobedience and failure to rely upon God, are vulnerable to being devoured. Satan wants to devour your marriage. Satan wants to devour your children. He wants to have them, and he wants the world to have them. He wants to bring reproach on the name of Christ. That's the battle in which each of us is engaged.

You say, "I don't want my family devoured!" Great, but the way that we think to stop Satan in his tracks is not God's way to do so. Our approach is to draw the line and stand our ground and raise our fists and stick up for our rights. The biblical way, the way to cooperate with what God is doing in this world, is the way of love. That is our protection.

Genesis 4 tells us that God put a mark on Cain, and he went his own way and wandered in the wilderness the rest of his life. The way of Cain is opposite to the way of love. People who take the way of Cain—the way of hatred instead of love—still wander in a wilderness and miss the good things of life that God desires to give to them. Do you want God's protection on your family? When we love in return for hate, when we turn the other cheek, when we go the second mile, we are avoiding the life of Cain. We are choosing the way of love, and we experience God's protection and covering over our family.

LOVE IS PROOF.

Love is also proof. First John 3:13–14: "**Do not be surprised, brethren, if the world hates you. We know that we have passed out of death into life, because we love the brethren.**" Who are the *brethren?* They are our brothers and sisters in Christ, at church and at home. They are people to whom we have made a long-term commitment—to love them through thick and thin, through ups and downs, and to keep on going together through life. People who make those kinds of commitments are proving something.

Do you see, in verse 14, what they are proving? "**We know that we have passed out of death into life.**" The love talked about in this passage conveys continuous action, continual loving. Jesus said in Luke 6:32 that if you only love people who love you—well, what's the big deal about that? Even sinners do that! No, the big deal is if you can love people that hate you, if you can love people that use you, if you can love people that neglect you. That's proving something! It proves that you have truly grasped the magnitude of Christ's love for you, and that you have passed from death to life.

HATRED IS MURDER.

The text goes on in verse 15: "**Everyone who hates his brother is a murderer; and you know that no murderer has eternal life abiding in him.**" Now why is hatred the same as murder? Because God looks at your heart, not just at your actions. He knows what He sees, and He sees everything. If you hate someone in your heart, then maybe you would kill him—except that you don't know how, or you haven't had a chance, or you are afraid you would go to prison. But you would if you had the right opportunity.

God says, "It's just the same to Me as if you did kill them. I am not looking at what you *do;* I don't have to. I am looking at what you *are* and what you *feel.*" If your heart is filled with hatred, you are a murderer. And no murderer has eternal life.

So here's the question. Do you truly know Jesus? Have you really turned from your sin and embraced Christ for your forgiveness? Do you have a personal relationship with Him? If you do, then you don't hate people. There should not be a single person whom you have known personally that you could not embrace, even if they were to sit down beside you this very moment.

You say, "People have hurt me." People have hurt me, too, and I have had to labor on my knees to get to a good place with them. That's where you need to be; it's the place of living according to love

IS YOUR LOVE GROWING?

Unquenchable, unconquerable, unstoppable love is proof that you really know the Savior. Verse 16: "**We know love by this, that He laid down His life**

for us; and we ought to lay down our lives for the brethren." If you truly know Christ, there will be a growing pattern of love in your life.

Are you growing in love? You say, "I was never really a loving person growing up. I didn't come from a very loving family." OK, but you are in Christ now. So are you growing in your capacity to love? Are the following statements true of you?

1. *I love more people than ever before.* How many people do you love? Think about it for a minute. Has the number increased since you became a follower of Jesus Christ? Can you honestly say, "I love the people who live on my street, and I love all the people at work. They don't always understand because they have their guard up, but I just do everything I can to serve them. I am growing in my love for my family. I never used to love my in-laws, but I have been growing in Christ, and things are changing." Listen, that's what the Christian life is all about. It's not just a matter of singing a few songs or memorizing a few Bible verses. If you are plugged into the Master, then you are growing in your capacity to love. And that means loving more people than ever before.

2. *I love more kinds of people than ever before.* Praise God, we have people from many different racial, cultural, and economic backgrounds attending Harvest Bible Chapel together. What a fantastic picture of the kingdom of Christ, where we are all one in Him! I pray often that the racial and cultural diversity of our church will exceed that of our surrounding community. We want to be known as a place where people are loved, not as a place where people are looked at and measured and assessed according to externals that don't matter to God. That's the world, not the kingdom of Christ. How are you doing in this? Are you growing in your capacity to love more kinds of people than ever before? You need to be.

3. *I love over longer periods of time than ever before.* You say, "When I first came to Christ, I could only put up with somebody for so long, and then I was like, 'I am so done with you!'" So much of the body of Christ is like that. The pastor moves on, and the people move on. How sad! What could be better than looking into the face of a person whom you have loved for many years and saying, "I am still loving you, brother! You are still loving me. We are in this together." That is what the love of

Christ is all about—persevering in love over longer periods of time than ever before.

PROVE IT AT HOME.

If that is your testimony, you're proving something. You're proving that you have passed from death unto life and that you know the One who laid down His life for us. Love is proof. And this kind of love is urgently needed in our marriages and with our children. Here's why: You can change your job—people do it all the time. You can change your neighborhood. I mean, if your neighbors are just driving you nuts, you can always move across town. And as much as it pains me to admit it, you can even change churches, though I am never in favor of that. But listen: You cannot change your family.

If ever there were a place where you needed a growing capacity for love, it's in the home. What else is going to allow you to love these people for the rest of your life? You are not getting a different wife! Your husband is with you for life! You think, *I'm sure I'd be happier if I could just make a change now and cut my losses.* You are kidding yourself! There is more pain in that decision than you could ever anticipate—and devastation for your loved ones. Stick it out. Persevere in love. Prove with your life that you really do know Jesus Christ. Don't give up on that person. Don't give up on that relationship.

Go back and humble yourself and say you're sorry. Start again. Get on your knees and pray for the love of Christ to permeate your marriage and your home and every relationship.

LOVE IS PRACTICAL.

This is not pie-in-the-sky stuff. This is as real as it gets. Love is practical.

Notice what it says in 1 John 3:17: **"But whoever has the world's goods, and sees his brother in need and closes his heart against him, how does the love of God abide in him?"** Can you picture the scenario being described here? Suppose you see a homeless man lying off by the side of the street. He tries like anything to make eye contact with you. He says something like, "Can you help? Do you have any money? Would you assist me?" What are you going to do? You might be tempted to close your heart toward him: *If I give him some money, he will just drink it away. How can I be sure he is not a con artist? Most* *likely, he has already rejected the help of his own family. Why should I help him?* These are the mental gymnastics of closing your heart to love.

Several years ago, the Lord dealt very strongly with me about this very thing. I have made a commitment to Him since that time, that, if I have anything in my wallet and I see a person in need, I will never—so help me, God— refuse to help them. Never! I have a lot of loving to do in this life, and I can't afford to close my heart when God is working to open it wider and wider. I must always be seeking to expand my capacity to love in practical ways.

Verse 18: "**Little children, let us not love with word or with tongue, but in deed and truth.**" I recently heard about a minister in our area who dressed up like a homeless person and laid on the sidewalk outside his church on Sunday morning. All of the people came in, and not one of them spoke to him. At the appropriate time, he walked up onto the platform, took off the costume he was wearing, and began to preach. Boy, did the people listen! Now, I don't mean to imply that love is only about helping people in that kind of acute need. My point is this: Your heart is either opening or closing to this concept of love. Don't think that you can fool God—He knows the truth.

If your heart is opening up to love, you will see every opportunity in your life as a chance to "**love [not just] with word or with tongue, but in deed and truth.**" Be ready to act out your love. Show it.

DEFINING LOVE

John Stott, a British pastor and scholar, wrote that, "Love is the willingness to surrender that which has value in our life to enrich the life of another." What a great definition! Giving up something that I value to enrich the life of someone else. That's love. But many people don't get this "enriching the life of another" stuff. They say, "I'll do these things for you, if you do these things for me." That's the typical marriage. The problem is that when the husband stops doing his part, the wife stops doing hers. There is nothing loving about that. That is merely a contractual relationship. Love says, "I am not counting what you're doing. I am not measuring and I am not keeping score. I am trying to enrich your life; I am spending myself so that your life can be better." That's love!

If you want the most practical definition of love, here it is: U B4 ME. It's like a license plate. Get it? "You before me." That's love. I must be concerned about what *you* need. Whether you are or are not concerned about what *I* need is a secondary matter. But I will say this: If you want a member of your family to be concerned about your needs—don't demand, don't throw a temper tantrum, don't nag—do your part and allow God to work through your actions to convict the other person about love.

That's what love does. It keeps on acting, keeps on waiting, keeps on working, and keeps on trusting God to produce the needed changes in others.

WHAT'S YOUR LOVE LANGUAGE?

Gary Chapman, best-selling author of *The Five Love Languages,* observed from his twenty years of counseling that, "Love has many dialects, but it has five main languages." In other words, there are different ways to communicate love to people. You could be trying to love someone, but if you are not speaking his or her love language, you might as well be speaking Swahili. The person just doesn't get it. And that can be a very confusing thing for people, especially within the family. I would suggest that the critical issue is not whether you love your kids or your spouse, but whether they feel loved. Are you getting the message through to them?

The key to seeing your love connect with a family member's heart is understanding his or her love language. Here are the big five:

1. *Words of affirmation.* That is how some people feel loved. "Thank you for making such a delicious dinner." "You look wonderful today." "I appreciate you so much." "I am so blessed to have discovered a wife like you!" To those whose love language is words of affirmation, such expressions clearly communicate love.

2. *Quality time.* This is my wife's love language. I can say nice things to her until the cows come home, but she is like, "I need time. Give me your attention. Tune in here." That is difficult for men sometimes. I have had to work hard on that over the years. As frequently as possible, we go on dates where we can shut out everything else and focus in on one another.

3. *Receiving gifts.* Perhaps you married a woman whose love language is receiving gifts. Well, what's your problem? Stop being such a cheapskate, and get on the program! A gift says you were thinking about her

when you weren't with her. It's not the gift but the thought that counts, as they say.

4. *Acts of service.* These show support and care for your family. Coming home early, helping with the children, ironing a shirt, making an extra-nice meal. For some people, an act of service communicates love.

5. *Physical touch.* A hug. A kiss. Holding hands. A pat on the shoulder. A meaningful gesture. All of these help you connect to the hearts of your family members.

I stand up at the front of our worship center after each of our three weekend services and talk to people as long as I am able. In doing so, I have learned a lot about love languages. You never know how a person will react. Sometimes I will step toward someone to give a hug, and the person's like, "Agh!" He turns into an oak tree, and I think, *Oops, obviously not his love language!* But other people respond with affection and a warm embrace. It just depends on the person. Loving people accommodate themselves to the love language of the person to whom they are trying to minister.

"Little children, let us not love with word or with tongue, but in deed and truth" (1 John 3:18). Love is practical.

LOVE IS PRODUCTIVE.

Love gets stuff done in our homes. Everyone knows by personal experience what is found in verses 19–20: **"We will know by this that we are of the truth, and will assure our heart before Him in whatever our heart condemns us."** Does your heart ever condemn you? It'll be like, "You are such a lousy Christian right now! I heard what you said at home." Or, "If you were a true Christian, you never would have let that thought enter your mind. You think you are so different? You have all the people at church fooled." So many believers hear thoughts like these—do you know what I'm talking about? It's your heart. It's not the Holy Spirit condemning you at that point; it's a weak, uninformed conscience.

When your conscience is accusing you, you **"will know by this that [you] are of the truth."** Know by *what?* By loving in deed and truth. A lifestyle of love will give us the assurance we need. So the next time your heart starts condemning you—"You are such a loser Christian!"—you can respond, "I am not what I *could be*, and I am not what I *should be*, but praise the Lord I am not what I was. I am a daughter of God. I am a son of the Father. I have a growing capacity to love. It doesn't matter what you say about me. God has set His love upon me. I am in process, and I am moving forward."

WHAT MATTERS IS WHAT GOD SAYS.

If that doesn't put an end to the condemnation, then notice the last part of verse 20: **"For God is greater than our heart and knows all things."** At the end of the day, it doesn't really matter what I say about myself. What matters is what God says about me and what His Word says about me. That's why it is so important for us to study God's Word regularly—so that we can know what it means to follow Christ and grow in Him. We don't have to have a weak, uninformed conscience that condemns us; we can have a growing understanding of the truth. So the next time you find yourself wondering, "Am I really a Christian?" just ask yourself this question, "Am I growing in love?" That's the bottom line. It is the greatest commandment.

In fact, Romans 13:10 says, **"Love is the fulfillment of the law."** Can you imagine that? What an incredible statement! But think about it: Why would you steal from someone if you loved him? Why would you commit adultery against someone if you loved him or her? Why would you take the name of the Lord your God in vain if you loved Him? Love is the fulfillment of the law.

THE CHRISTIAN LIFE REALLY WORKS.

"Beloved, if our heart does not condemn us, we have confidence before God; and whatever we ask we receive from Him, because we keep His commandments and do the things that are pleasing in His sight" (1 John 3:21–22). Notice the pattern:

- The more I love, the more confidence I have.
- The more confidence I have, the more I pray.
- The more I pray, the more I see answers to prayer.
- The more I see answers to prayer, the more I want to keep living for God.

This Christian life thing really works. And it all starts with love. Love leads to confidence; confidence leads to prayer; prayer leads to answers; answers to more obedience. Love fuels the whole thing. Love is productive.

LOVE IS PRIORITY NUMBER ONE.

Love is priority number one. Look at verse 23: **"This is His commandment, that we believe in the name of His Son Jesus Christ, and love one another, just as He commanded us."** How clear could that be?

Consider for a moment everything we've studied together in this book. All of it—*all of it*—flows from love. How could you possibly forgive someone unless you love them? Why would you bless your children or honor your parents apart from love? Truth—it's love's greatest ally. The local church is the place where you practice love to others. And commitments are kept only because of love.

You say, "James, I don't have this kind of love." I am so glad you can admit that. Only when we recognize that we don't have this kind of love can we begin to understand that it comes only from a relationship with Christ. It is the cross of Christ, the perfect example of love, which enables us to live a life of love. **"This is His commandment, that we believe in the name of His Son Jesus Christ, and love one another."** Go after this love for yourself and for your family, and it will transform you.

A PRAYER TO GO HIGHER

→→ ←←

Lord, thank You for Your cross of love. Thank You for Your nail-pierced hands and feet, and for the blood that flowed from Your side. What a picture of sacrificial love! Lord, draw me close to Your cross, and remind me of what it means to give and to spend myself for others. Forgive me for my selfish, sinful ways, and cause me afresh to be a person of love.

Lord, make me the most loving person in my family. God, make me the most loving person in my marriage. Cause me to stop keeping score all the time. Give me persevering love, not just when things are wonderful and delightful, but also when they are difficult and frustrating. May Your cross stir within me a supernatural capacity to love my family. Help me to see love as the transforming influence that it is.

Lord Jesus, thank You for being my example. I pray this in Your name. Amen.

A PROJECT TO GO DEEPER

Love is a proof of authentic discipleship. The apostle John repeatedly drives home this point in his first letter. Read through the entire book of 1 John and jot down the verses that contribute to this important theme. Summarize your findings in one or two succinct statements, and then reflect upon your own experience. How does your life measure up to God's standards in this matter of love? What action steps can you take to better prove the authenticity of your commitment to Christ?

A PRACTICE TO GO FURTHER

Go back and reread the section on the five love languages. Think about each member of your immediate family—your spouse, kids, parents, siblings. Can you identify the primary love language for each of them? If you're finding it difficult to pinpoint someone's love language, sit down with that person and talk about it. Find out how that family member likes to receive love.

Once you've figured out everyone's language, go out of your way within the week to love each of your family members in his or her primary language. Surprise them all. Knock their socks off. Blow them away. Do something that you have never done before. And then . . . keep on doing it!

GIVING THE
BLESSING

The "Practice to Go Further" that concludes chapter 3 calls on you to design a chart to evaluate how you are doing on giving a blessing. Feel free to use the chart shown on the next page to do this; you may even photocopy the chart for your own use. Remember the children may be your own and/or nieces or nephews, younger cousins, kids you teach in the children's program at church, neighborhood kids. Reflect upon your interactions with each of them. How are you doing at conveying the blessing to each child? What can you do to communicate the blessing with greater purpose in each of the five ways?

WAYS TO GIVE THE BLESSING

Name	Meaningful Touch	Spoken Words	Affirming Value	Spiritual Vision	Prosperous Vision
1.					
2.					
3.					
4.					
5.					
6.					
7.					

SAMPLE
TRIBUTES

→► ◄←

The "Practice to Go Further" that concludes chapter 4 calls on you to write a formal tribute to each of your parents. In addition to the suggestions offered in that chapter for writing a tribute, here are two sample tributes. They are the tributes I wrote and spoke to my parents just a few years ago.

A Tribute to Lorna May Sherwood MacDonald

Dear Mom,

For several months, no, really for years, I have been forming in my mind words of honor and tribute to you for being such an incredible mother and investing your very best in me. As adults, we see things kids never see, and that perspective has only heightened my respect of and gratitude for the woman God chose to be my mother.

You are far too loyal a person to ever say so, but I know you overcame many challenges as a child that I never faced. Instead of the support I received through all my school years, you had to quit high school to help support your parents. I remember you saying, "Sherwoods know how to work." You sure did, and do, and you taught me to love and value hard work. You overcame other obstacles, too. Your parents were not as emotive or expressive with their love as they should have been. God knows why, but you did not use that as an excuse. You always say you knew that they loved you, but I have known and heard and felt your love. Your parents needed to labor six days a week to make ends meet, and they moved every year. I had the advantage of available parents, long-term friendships, and eighteen years in the same house and church. You were the first to choose Jesus in your family, and then led your parents to salvation. I had parents who told me about Jesus before I could walk. Mom, you are an overcomer in a world of excuse makers. May I be like you?

Remember the countless Bible clubs on Tuesdays after school? Our basement jammed with kids to hear about Jesus through flannel board stories—you are such a great teacher and storyteller! Remember the neighbor ladies over for coffee, and the ones you led to Christ? Doing friendship evangelism years before anyone was talking about it. Remember leading me to Christ—kneeling by my bed, your red Bible, your arms around me, praying with me. Did you cry?

It wasn't all spiritual, though, was it, Mom? I know I often *made* you cry. Remember how hard I tried to kill myself—or so it must have seemed. Ten trips to the emergency room before I was twelve, seventy-five stitches in increments of seven, a broken wrist, a broken collarbone, a broken nose—it's a wonder you didn't break my neck!

Remember when you threw the knife at me at dinner? . . . Remember when you threw the tea on me at dinner? . . . Remember the times you sent me to my room without dinner? . . . It all makes sense now.

Corn chowder and scallop potatoes, donuts and peanut butter cookies, popcorn balls and apple crisp. Paper routes and baseball teams and basketball—constantly. Youth retreats, and school events, and birthday parties. Four boys and you did it all. I used to wonder why you slept on Sunday afternoons. . . . Now I know.

Remember how I'd make you laugh, cry, occasionally swear, and always pray. You were never perfect but always authentic, hating hypocrisy the most. I hope I am like you in that.

You raised me good, you taught me well, you walked your talk, you let me go. From a distance, you're still loving, still cheering, still supporting, still praying.

I honor you, Mom! You are a triple double, grand slam, record-setting mother—a success by faith. I hear you saying, "For His glory, James," and I say AMEN.

A Tribute to Verne Hubert MacDonald

Dear Dad,

Ephesians 6:2 commands us to "honor your father and mother." Since the day I wrote that tribute to Mom, I have been forming in my mind similar words of tribute to you, waiting for the right time to share them with you. Today is that day.

Much of what a man is and becomes arrives through his dad, and as I scan the landscape of my heritage, I see beyond you and before you. I see a grand-father and a great-grandfather who are at this moment in the presence of the Lord, and I praise God that I can stand in a line of men who have loved and served God faithfully and found Him to be a shelter in their generation.

Dad, my mind is racing as I think of all you have given me. Thanks for working so hard to provide: for carrying Coke cases, and buying and selling cars, and teaching summer school, and getting your master's degree, and let-ting Mom be at home with us.

Thanks for giving me a love for history. Reading historical plaques while we yawned and fidgeted. Rummaging through old homesteads in search of an-tique bottles, loading me down with books about the pioneer days, taking me to Arthur Ford School during the Christmas holidays so I could do my pro-ject on James Watt.

Thanks for letting me get C's in school when you wanted so much more and protecting my will to learn until I was ready to use it. Remember driving me to summer school and going to my teachers to fight for me when you thought I deserved a break? Remember the day we argued about study hall—"a lawyer in the making," you thought? Remember the night I threw my math books at the wall and cried, how you kept your cool and listened?

Thanks for teaching me to love my wife: by loving Mom in front of us; by arguing and yelling and kissing and making up right before our little eyes; by making sure we knew that your love for Mom came first; by insisting that we treated her with the same respect you did. I'll never forget the time I screamed at Mom and ran from the house, and how when I came home you sat me down and scolded me and cried and read the Bible to me and prayed for God to change my heart.

Thanks for stale donuts on Saturday night, and for teaching us that if you know who you are you can dress any way you want and not really care. Thanks for camping and convertibles, for catch in the backyard and construction projects, for cow auctions and the cottage, for corporal punishment and caring conversation, for calling a spade a spade and calling us home for dinner.

Thanks for leading our family spiritually. Thanks for taking us back to church on Sunday nights and Wednesdays, for leading singing at Thamesford Baptist Church, for being the Sunday School superintendent, for going to church clean-up days, and for standing in front of the whole church while Mom trembled to sing "Through It All" and "The King Is Coming." Thanks for loving the church.

Dad, I could write all day about the things you have given me, but I have to get home and stuff the turkey. One final word of thanks says it all: Thanks for getting past religion and ritual to a real thing with God. Thanks for loving Jesus Christ in a growing, personal, authentic, faithful, contagious way. Thanks for transmitting that love for Christ to your sons and now to your grandchildren. I honor you, Dad, for you are worthy of double honor. I do not know, nor have ever met, a man I would be more proud to call my father, and I pray, for the glory of Christ alone, that I can be half the man to my kids that you have been and are to me.

Your son,
James

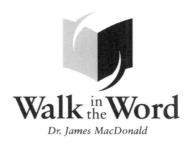

Walk in the Word

Dr. James MacDonald

Igniting Passion in the People of God Through the Proclamation of Truth

Walk in the Word is the teaching ministry of Dr. James MacDonald. Pastor James has been in ministry for over 15 years. Originally from Canada, James and his wife, Kathy, have three children and make their home in suburban Chicago. He is senior pastor at Harvest Bible Chapel, one of the fastest growing churches in the Chicago area with a congregation of more than 5,000 worshippers.

The ministry of Walk in the Word is based on Isaiah 30:21, "Whether you turn to the right or to the left, your ears will hear a voice behind you saying, 'This is the way; walk in it.'" (NIV)

Much of the preaching in our day rightly aims at the mind and brings teaching and instruction to dispel ignorance. Other ministries focus on meeting the obvious need for biblical encouragement in the hearts of the Lord's people.

While not neglecting these important areas, Walk in the Word seeks to challenge the will. Our goal is to ignite passion in the people of God through the proclamation of truth. Never has the Word of God been so readily available and made such little difference in the way people live. It isn't enough just to hear the Word. We must actually "do what it says" (James 1:22).

Pastor James' teaching is available through his daily radio program called Walk in the Word, now heard on more than 400 stations as well as the internet where it is available 24 hours a day, seven days a week. In addition to numerous books, booklets, and magazine articles, Walk in the Word distributes thousands of audio tapes and CDs each year.

For more information on the ministry of Walk in the Word please contact us at 1-888-581-WORD (9673) or on the internet at www.WalkintheWord.com. Our e-mail address is letters@WalkintheWord.com, and our mailing address is P.O. Box 764, Arlington Heights, IL 60006, or in Canada P.O. Box 324, Markham, ON L3P 3J8.

More from James MacDonald and Moody Press

LORD, CHANGE MY ATTITUDE
(Before It's Too Late)

Attitudes, says author and pastor James MacDonald, are patterns of thinking that take years to form. While we can't change our attitudes overnight, we can recognize wrong attitudes and begin working on right attitudes to take their place.

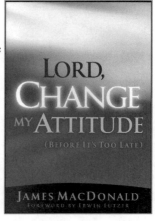

"When James MacDonald speaks, I lean forward in my chair to catch every word. He communicates the Word of God with a deep commitment to the truth and with great understanding of the people who hear him. He makes you want to hear what God has said, and, better still, you find yourself wanting to do it."
— Dr. David Jeremiah, Turning Point Ministries

ISBN: 0-8024-3442-8

I REALLY WANT TO CHANGE . . .
So, Help Me God

Change is never easy. Sometimes it's downright painful. But because we are called as believers in Christ to holiness, we simply can't stay as we are. This is a book about how to achieve a different you. It includes study questions, exercises, and prayers that lead to change.

"This is the ideal book for people who are serious about seeing lasting changes take place in their character and conduct. The author is both compassionate and confrontational—no kid gloves! You will either read it through and honestly put it into practice or you will invent another excuse for staying as you are."

— Warren Weirsbe, Author and Conference Speaker

ISBN: 0-8024-3423-1

MOODY
The Name You Can Trust
1-800-678-8812 **www.MoodyPress.org**